Creating concrete5 Themes

Create high quality concrete5 themes using
practical recipes and responsive techniques
to make it mobile-ready

Remo Laubacher

PUBLISHING

BIRMINGHAM - MUMBAI

Creating concrete5 Themes

First published: January 2013

Production Reference: 1210113

Published by Packt Publishing Ltd.
Livery Place
35 Livery Street
Birmingham B3 2PB, UK.

ISBN 978-1-78216-164-6

www.packtpub.com

Cover Image by Suresh Mogre (suresh.mogre.99@gmail.com)

Credits

Author
Remo Laubacher

Reviewer
Naume Keculovski

James Shannon

Acquisition Editor
Mary Jasmine Nadar

Commissioning Editor
Yogesh Dalvi

Technical Editors
Vrinda Amberkar

Charmaine Pereira

Pooja Prakashan

Lubna Shaikh

Hardik Soni

Copy Editor
Alfida Paiva

Aditya Nair

Ruta Waghmare

Project Coordinator
Amigya Khurana

Proofreader
Samantha Lyon

Indexer
Hemangini Bari

Graphics
Valentina D'silva

Aditi Gajjar

Production Coordinator
Prachali Bhiwandkar

Cover Work
Prachali Bhiwandkar

About the Author

Remo Laubacher grew up in Central Switzerland in a small village surrounded by mountains and natural beauty. He started working with computers a long time ago and then, after various computer related projects, he focused on ERP and Oracle development. After completing his BSc in Business Administration, Remo became a partner at Ortic, his ERP and Oracle business, as well as a partner at mesch web consulting and design GmbH. At mesch – where he's responsible for all development related topics – he discovered concrete5 as the perfect tool for their web-related projects and has since become a key member of the concrete5 community. You can find his latest publications at `http://www.codeblog.ch/`.

About the Reviewer

Naume Keculovski was born in 1983 in Macedonia, but grew up in a small village close to Zurich, Switzerland. After getting his EFZ degree with a focus on Application Development, he started working for a small company and gained his first practical web development experience. After finishing his internship, he started working for mesch and now builds the best possible web solutions on top of concrete5, with Remo Laubacher.

James Shannon has been actively developing with concrete5 since its early days. He's contributed to the core and built a number of c5-powered sites, but mostly uses it as a framework to build complex web applications. Additionally, he's released a handful of popular packages that augment concrete5's core functionality. More generally, he's been developing websites for 15 years using a number of technologies.

James' professional expertise is in strategic project management and change management.

James grew up in Southern California and graduated from UC Berkeley. He collects certifications, most recently one that allows him to fly planes.

I'd like to thank the person most important to me, Julie Talone, and the one most important to her, Henry.

www.PacktPub.com

Support files, eBooks, discount offers and more

You might want to visit www.PacktPub.com for support files and downloads related to your book.

Did you know that Packt offers eBook versions of every book published, with PDF and ePub files available? You can upgrade to the eBook version at www.PacktPub.com and as a print book customer, you are entitled to a discount on the eBook copy. Get in touch with us at service@packtpub.com for more details.

At www.PacktPub.com, you can also read a collection of free technical articles, sign up for a range of free newsletters and receive exclusive discounts and offers on Packt books and eBooks.

http://PacktLib.PacktPub.com

Do you need instant solutions to your IT questions? PacktLib is Packt's online digital book library. Here, you can access, read and search across Packt's entire library of books.

Why Subscribe?

- Fully searchable across every book published by Packt
- Copy and paste, print and bookmark content
- On demand and accessible via web browser

Free Access for Packt account holders

If you have an account with Packt at www.PacktPub.com, you can use this to access PacktLib today and view nine entirely free books. Simply use your login credentials for immediate access.

Table of Contents

Preface

The *Creating concrete5 Themes* book contains everything you'll need to use your experience with HTML, CSS, and PHP, to build custom themes for concrete5. You'll also get a first glimpse at more advanced features as well as a few examples showing you how to customize parts of the concrete5 core to uncover the power of this CMS.

What this book covers

Chapter 1, Getting Started, describes a few words about the requirements of concrete5 as well as instructions needed to get an understanding to edit content using concrete5.

Chapter 2, Architecture of concrete5, helps you understand a bit more about the internals of concrete5 for those who want to understand how things are working in concrete5.

Chapter 3, Creating Your First Theme, describes the practical part where you'll create your own theme.

Chapter 4, Styling Single Page, helps you learn how to change the look of existing pages such as the login or 404 page.

Chapter 5, Styling the Block Output, covers everything you need to know to change the output of the block elements, the actual content of a concrete5 site.

Chapter 6, Responsive Themes, covers a brief look into responsive techniques and how they can be integrated in concrete5.

What you need for this book

You'll need an environment where you can install and play around with concrete5. This can either be a Windows, Mac, or Linux computer with Apache, PHP, and MySQL, or even a remote server in combination with a text editor such as Notepad++ and a tool to upload files such as FileZilla.

Who this book is for

You don't need to be an experienced programmer to understand this book, but you should have an understanding of web technologies such as HTML and CSS. Some experience with a programming language, preferably PHP, is highly recommended, but not needed if you are a quick learner with a good understanding of computers.

Conventions

In this book, you will find a number of styles of text that distinguish between different kinds of information. Here are some examples of these styles, and an explanation of their meaning.

Code words in text are shown as follows: "The value of `$pkg` has to match the package directory and `theme_book` in `PageTheme::add('theme_book', $pkg);` has to match the name of the theme directory in `themes`."

A block of code is set as follows:

```php
<?php
$mh = Loader::helper('mail');
$mh->setSubject('Hello lovely World');
$mh->setBody('Have a great day!');
$mh->to('the@world.org', 'The World');
$mh->from('me@switzerland.ch');
$mh->sendMail();
```

When we wish to draw your attention to a particular part of a code block, the relevant lines or items are set in bold:

```
<div class="span9">
        <?php
        $areaMain = new Area('Main');
        $areaMain->display($c);
        ?>
</div>
```

New terms and **important words** are shown in bold. Words that you see on the screen, in menus or dialog boxes for example, appear in the text like this: "There are some links such as **Add Image** which are concrete5 specific."

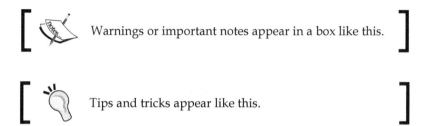

> Warnings or important notes appear in a box like this.

> Tips and tricks appear like this.

Reader feedback

Feedback from our readers is always welcome. Let us know what you think about this book—what you liked or may have disliked. Reader feedback is important for us to develop titles that you really get the most out of.

To send us general feedback, simply send an e-mail to feedback@packtpub.com, and mention the book title via the subject of your message.

If there is a topic that you have expertise in and you are interested in either writing or contributing to a book, see our author guide on www.packtpub.com/authors.

Customer support

Now that you are the proud owner of a Packt book, we have a number of things to help you to get the most from your purchase.

Downloading the example code

You can download the example code files for all Packt books you have purchased from your account at http://www.PacktPub.com. If you purchased this book elsewhere, you can visit http://www.PacktPub.com/support and register to have the files e-mailed directly to you.

Errata

Although we have taken every care to ensure the accuracy of our content, mistakes do happen. If you find a mistake in one of our books — maybe a mistake in the text or the code — we would be grateful if you would report this to us. By doing so, you can save other readers from frustration and help us improve subsequent versions of this book. If you find any errata, please report them by visiting http://www.packtpub.com/support, selecting your book, clicking on the **errata submission form** link, and entering the details of your errata. Once your errata are verified, your submission will be accepted and the errata will be uploaded on our website, or added to any list of existing errata, under the Errata section of that title. Any existing errata can be viewed by selecting your title from http://www.packtpub.com/support.

Piracy

Piracy of copyright material on the Internet is an ongoing problem across all media. At Packt, we take the protection of our copyright and licenses very seriously. If you come across any illegal copies of our works, in any form, on the Internet, please provide us with the location address or website name immediately so that we can pursue a remedy.

Please contact us at copyright@packtpub.com with a link to the suspected pirated material.

We appreciate your help in protecting our authors, and our ability to bring you valuable content.

Questions

You can contact us at questions@packtpub.com if you are having a problem with any aspect of the book, and we will do our best to address it.

1
Getting Started

concrete5 is a powerful content management system which is not only easy to use, but also powerful when you want to customize the look of a site and extend it with functionality. In this chapter, we'll start by looking at concrete5 from the user side. You'll learn about the basic ideas behind concrete5 as well as its most used tools to manage your site and content as you go.

Getting your own concrete5 site

If you already have a site of your own, you can skip this part. For those without a concrete5 site, you can start by checking out the trial option on the official site: `http://www.concrete5.org/about/trial/`. On this site, you can get your demo site up and running with just a few clicks. There is no need to download, install, or configure anything. While this is perfectly fine to get acquainted with concrete5, you won't be able to change the files of the system. If you want to get a first impression, go for it, but if you want to play around with the code and layout of your site, make sure you get your own site up and running.

In case you want to run your own site, there are official hosting packages where you get your concrete5 installation without any worries. Check the different packages here:

`http://www.concrete5.org/services/hosting/`

As concrete5 is an open source CMS, you can, of course, run everything on your own server. The most-used platform is definitely LAMP (Linux, Apache, MySQL, and PHP). There are a lot of people who run concrete5 on different platforms such as Microsoft IIS. While it's usually not a problem to get concrete5 running as long as the platform supports PHP and MySQL, LAMP is the only officially-supported platform. If possible, make sure you work with Apache on Linux as it's also the platform where you're most likely to get support in case something doesn't work as expected.

You can find information about the installation process, as well as a number of tutorials for different platforms, on the following page:

```
http://www.concrete5.org/documentation/installation/installing_
concrete5/
```

Quick installation guide for those who have worked with PHP web applications before:

- You'll need a working LAMP environment.
- You need to download the latest stable version from the following page: `http://www.concrete5.org/developers/downloads/`.
- Extract all of the files to a temporary folder on your computer.
- Use an FTP client, such as FileZilla, to upload all of these files to your web server. Make sure `index.php` is in the folder from which you want to serve your site (for example, `http://www.your-site.com/`).
- Open that URL in your browser, you'll be shown a screen where you can enter the administrator's credentials as well as the information needed to connect to the database. Put the correct values in each field and confirm them by clicking on the **Install concrete5** button.

Start working with concrete5

Once you have a running concrete5 site, you can log in to your site by clicking on the **Sign In to Edit this Site** link at the bottom of the page. If you already installed a different theme, you might not find that link, as some people remove it to keep their layout as clean as possible. If that's the case, you can use the following URL, or if that's not working either, the second URL:

- `http://www.your-site.com/login/`
- `http://www.your-site.com/index.php/login/`

Keeping URLs nice and clean

The two preceding links point to the same page but one has an ugly `index.php` in it. That's because all requests are redirected through that file. Luckily, it's not difficult to get rid of that. concrete5 can make use of `mod_rewrite` that makes it possible to remove parts of the URL.

In the dashboard, enter `pretty` in the little search bar at the top of the page and select the **Pretty URLs** item. On the screen which appears, check the only checkbox and save the changes. This is shown in the following screenshot:

After you're logged in, you'll see an almost identical view of your site, there's just one major change. Now there's a toolbar at the top, allowing you to access the dashboard as well as the editing options related to the current page:

Dashboard to manage concrete5

While you edit most of the content of a concrete5 site in the in-site editing mode, there's still a dashboard where you can manage a lot of different things. If you want to create a new user, group, manage your files, or change some permission, this is where you want to go.

The dashboard has two parts, a small part where you can see the most-used functions. Just hover over the **Dashboard** button and it will show up:

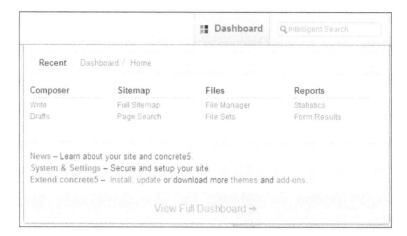

At the bottom, there's a **View Full Dashboard** link which will show you the entire dashboard. You can also get to the same screen by clicking on the **Dashboard** button at the top. The entire **Dashboard** screen is shown in the following screenshot:

If you like to explore things on your own, go on and click around to get familiar with the dashboard. We'll cover some parts of it in this book as we need them, but we aren't going to look at every single option, as this would be a topic for a whole book itself.

Managing dashboard favorites

In each screen of the dashboard, you'll find an icon looking like a star at the top-right corner, seen in the following screenshot. If you click on it, you'll mark that screen as a favorite. All of those screens will be listed in the dashboard menu which appears when you hover over the **Dashboard** button. This makes it easier to access often-used functions.

How to edit content

This is the part where concrete5 differs a lot from most classic content management systems. Many traditional systems have a clear distinction between the frontend and backend.

If you edit content by selecting the object you'd like to amend in a tree-like structure and see some fields structured like a database application you'll see a different concept. There's an in-site editing mode in concrete5 where you can update almost any content in a layout which looks a lot like the actual site, thus making it easier to actually understand the changes you're making.

You've already seen the toolbar at the top of every page. As you might have expected, the **Edit** button is what we need. The button has a menu which appears if you just hover over it. You'll see a small panel where you have a few functions to use, as seen below:

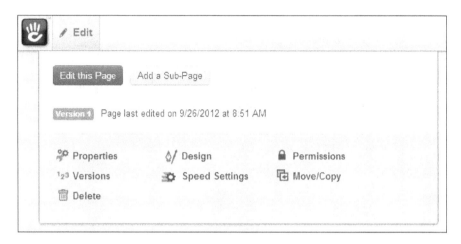

We'll use some of them later in this book, but to give you a first impression about what's here, the following is a short explanation for each item:

- **Edit this Page**: You want to change the content and not just look at it? Click on this button.

- **Add a Sub-Page**: This is the button you need if you want a new page underneath the current page. There's another way to manage the structure of your site, which we'll look at later in this chapter.

- **Properties**: A page has properties, such as a name or a meta description used by search engines as well as custom properties, for example, a background color you want to add to change the color per page. We'll create our own custom attribute later in this book.

- **Versions**: Once you change some content, concrete5 will automatically create a new version. This feature allows you to see all previous versions and even offers you the ability to compare them and go back to an older version.

- **Delete**: You don't need that page anymore? Delete it! You can restore pages that you've accidentally deleted in the site map. Display system pages there and you'll find an item called **trash** where you'll find the deleted pages.

- **Design**: A page can have different layouts, single column, two columns, and a lot more. This is where you can change the layout. We'll also create some of them later in this book.

- **Speed Settings**: There's a lot of caching functionality in concrete5 to improve the performance. Unless you have a big and complex site, leave these settings the way they are.

- **Permissions**: If you want to hide your vacation photos, concrete5 lets you easily set permissions to keep things private.

- **Move/Copy**: In case you want the current page to appear somewhere else on your site.

What are blocks

In concrete5, you can insert many different elements, starting from simple HTML content to videos and even small games by using **blocks**. There's pretty much no limit with blocks.

In other words, almost all content you place on your site is wrapped using a block. When someone wants you to add a picture, you'll need to select a block. If you want to add a guestbook, you need to insert a block.

You can see a list of all installed blocks if you navigate to `http://www.your-site.com/index.php/dashboard/blocks/types/`. To get you a quick overview, here's a list of all the default blocks, including a small description of their basic usage:

- `Auto-Nav`: This is what you need to add navigation to your site. By using this block, you make sure that new pages automatically appear in the navigation once you add them to the sitemap.

- `Content`: Probably the most used block, based on the HTML editor TinyMCE, this allows you to add formatted text, including links to other pages as well as embedded pictures. There are plans to replace TinyMCE with Redactor, but TinyMCE will probably be kept in the code to maintain backward compatibility.

- `Date Navigation`: This block groups a specified set of pages by their date, mostly useful for blog-like sites.

- `External Form`: If you need a custom form you can use this block, but please note, you'll need to write PHP code to actually use it.

- `File`: You can add links to files using the `Content` block as well, but if you just want one file download, this block is easier to use.

- `Flash Content`: Not very popular these days, but if you still want to embed your Flash file, use this block.

- `Form`: In addition to the `External Form` block, this block allows you to build a basic form without any knowledge of web technology such as PHP or JavaScript.

- `Google Map`: Add this block, supply an address, and your website visitors will be able to see where you live on a well-known Google map.

- `Guestbook/Comments`: This block provides a traditional guestbook, mostly used in blog posts, to allow your visitors to post comments. Includes e-mail notification as well as an approval functionality if required.

- `HTML`: For those of you who still want to hack their own HTML snippets into some pages. This block shows you a simple text area to enter your HTML code and nothing else.

- `Image`: This block allows you to add a picture with an optional on-state picture as well as the option to scale it.

- `Next & Previous Nav`: This block consists of a basic navigation to jump to the next page in the sitemap or chronological order.

- `Page List`: Unlike the `Auto-Nav` block, this block builds a flat list by using several filter options. It has two major usages:

  ◦ List all pages of a certain type (for example, all news pages to build an overview of the latest updates).

  ◦ List all pages underneath a page to build a simple sub-navigation.

- `RSS Displayer`: Fetches the latest updates from another site by using an RSS feed.

- `Search`: Inserts a search block with which you can run a full-text search across your site. Please note that you need to run a job to index the content of your site! Type `jobs` in the intelligent search box, if you click on the first result, you'll find a screen where you can execute several jobs (the search indexer included).

- `Slideshow`: This block helps display several pictures as a slideshow. You can also add a link to each slide, allowing your visitor to navigate away to a subpage by clicking on a slide.

- `Survey`: Want to find out if your visitors like the new desert recipe you've just posted? Add this block and you'll get the answer in no time!

- `Tags`: When building a blog, you usually assign tags to each post. By using this block, you can list all of the tags and find posts connected to them.

- `Video Player`: Have a look at this block if you want to embed a video on your site.

- `YouTube Video`: If you want to insert a video which is hosted on YouTube, use this block and your visitors get access to your favorite YouTube videos.

- `Blog Date Archive:` Much like the `Date Navigation` block, but it doesn't display the actual page/post and just links to an overview page where all of the matching pages are shown.

Getting more blocks from the marketplace

If you look on the screen where you can see all of the installed block types, there's also a button called **More Add-ons**. When you click on this button, you're asked to connect your site to the `concrete5.org marketplace`. This is a step you just need to do once per site. After that, you can access the list of add-ons right from the site and install more blocks if needed.

What is an area?

In concrete5, you don't specify where a picture or HTML text belongs; you simply define where the content managed by the user is located. A place where content can be placed is called an **area**.

If you look at the following screenshot, you'll see red rectangles marking a block. There are three blocks, one in the main area and two in the sidebar area. At the bottom, there are **Add To Main** and **Add To Sidebar** links. These links are part of the areas that let you add new blocks.

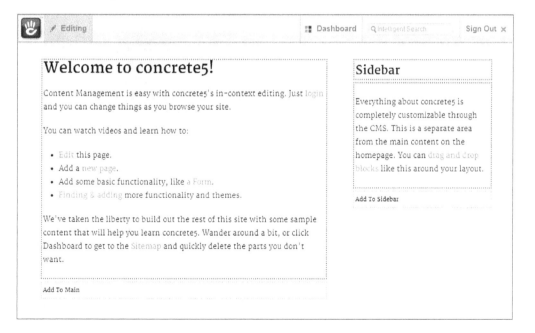

Adding and updating blocks

While you might want to look at all of the different options, this part is the one you and your clients need the most. Let's change the heading of the home page! If you're not in edit mode yet, click on the **Edit** button and the layout will change, as explained in the earlier paragraph.

Another change is shown when you click on an existing block. Each block has a menu where you can see a few options:

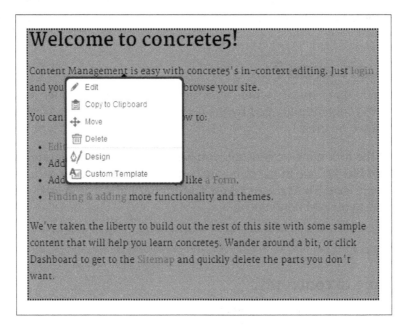

What are these options? They are explained as follows:

- **Edit**: This is obviously the menu item you need to edit your block. Each block has a different interface where you can update its content. There's an example after this list.

- **Copy to Clipboard**: This is like the clipboard you have in your operating system, but it's not connected to it. It basically copies an instance of a block into a holding place which you can later use to insert a new block with the same content on another page.

- **Move**: Each area can have several blocks and sometimes you want to change their order. This menu item changes the interface to a different mode where you can rearrange your blocks. You can also move a block from one area to another.

- **Delete**: This menu item removes blocks from the page.

- **Design**: This menu item lets you use some CSS-design features to change the border, alignment, font, color, and more.
- **Custom Template**: Each block has at least one template which is responsible for its output. However, a block can have more than one template which allows you to change the output in no time.

As we go on, we'll create our own templates for existing blocks to change the appearance, but for now, we'll just look at the basic editing function.

If you click on the block where the heading is, you'll see the preceding menu. Click on the **Edit** menu item and a new dialog pops up:

This dialog looks different for pretty much each block type, as most blocks have a different purpose as well. However, almost all of the blocks are easy to understand, and someone who has worked with computers for a while should be able to use them without any instructions.

The **Content** block you can see in the preceding screenshot is using TinyMCE to give you a word processor-like interface. Compared to the default TinyMCE editor, there's just one change on the top. There are some links such as **Add Image** which are concrete5-specific. They allow you to embed an image from the concrete5 file manager as well as add a link to another page of your site.

After you've changed the heading or content according to your needs, click on the **Save** button and you'll see the changes within the page layout. At this point, the changes are visible to you, but as they aren't published yet, website visitors won't see them.

Adding a new block is pretty much the same, you look for the area where you want to add a new block. If you want to add another content block to the sidebar, click on the **Add To Sidebar** link, as shown on the following screenshot:

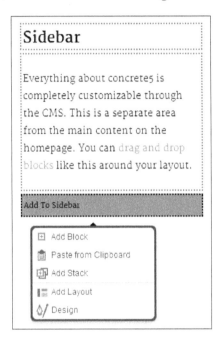

You'll see a list of all available blocks. Pick the **Content** block and you'll see the same block interface again, but this time without any content in it. Enter everything you need and confirm it by clicking on the **Add** button.

Publishing changes and managing versions

Once you've updated your content, you probably want to publish the changes at some point. You can leave the edited page without publishing it, keeping a draft version of the changes, but let's look at how you can make the changes available to the public. The toolbar at the top changes a bit when you're editing a page. The **Edit** button changes its text to **Editing** and a few elements in the menu underneath it change as well to make it possible to publish the changes:

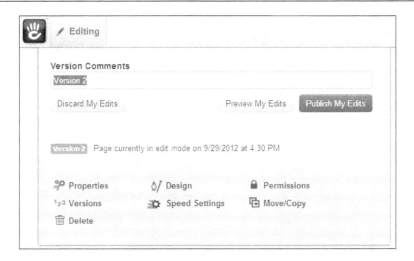

The button that jumps out at your eyes the quickest is the one you'll probably use the most in this situation. The **Publish My Edits** button will automatically make all of your changes available to the public. If you want to keep track of your changes, you can also replace the default text **Version 2** with a comment of your own. It's just a comment which will be listed when looking at previous versions, it doesn't have any functionality connected to it.

The other two buttons that are only visible in the edit mode are:

- **Discard My Edits**: Made a mistake and don't want to save the changes at all? Use this button.

- **Preview My Edits**: This button will save the changes but not approve them. Logged in editors can see and choose to continue editing, but normal users only see the approved version.

If you accidentally published a change you didn't want to release yet, don't worry, there's an easy way back! In the menu shown in the preceding screenshot, click on the **Versions** link and a new dialog will show up:

There are four buttons available:

- **1**: This is the compare versions button. If you select two or more page versions, this button will become active and shows you every selected version within a tab in a new dialog.

- **2**: This is the approve button. Select a version which isn't approved at the moment (including older versions) , and this button will be active, allowing you to change the publicly-visible page version. Thanks to this button, there's always an easy way back.

- **3**: This is the copy version button. Select one version and this button will make it possible to copy an existing version into a new one.

- **4**: This is the delete button. Select a page version that isn't approved at the moment and this button allows you to delete the selected version.

Managing files

A site without any pictures or files could look a bit boring, but luckily we have plenty of options to change that. If you navigate to the dashboard, you can see a **File Manager** link which will forward you to the default file manager screen in concrete5:

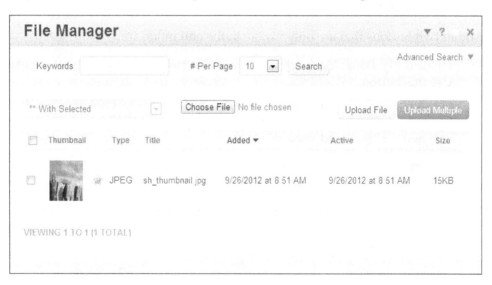

If you're used to working with another CMS, you'll probably have worked with a hierarchical folder structure known from most operating systems. In concrete5, things work a bit differently. You don't have folders, but rather *sets* in which you can place files. You can build a completely flat structure, but try to think about the sets you'll need before you have tons of files.

Unlike folders, a single file can be a part of several sets. This might sound a bit unusual, but once you're used to it, you'll probably realize that this can have advantages.

Uploading files

Let's have a look at how the usual process to upload a new file works. Right at the beginning we have two options. If you want to upload several files, you might want to use the **Upload Multiple** button where you can select as many files as you want and upload them in one bulk operation.

We'll use the traditional single file upload. Start by clicking on the **Choose File** button and select the file you want to upload from your local hard drive. After that, you only need to click on the **Upload File** button and you'll see another dialog where you can update the metadata of your new file:

If you click on one of the attributes such as **Title**, you'll see an input field where you can update the attribute value. Click on the icon on the right-hand side to confirm the changes to the value.

There are more attributes in the second tab, **Other Properties**. They all work the same way. Click on the attribute name, update the value, and confirm the change by clicking on the icon.

In the last tab **Sets**, you have the option to assign your new file to an existing set as well as a new set which you can create there as well. If you upload multiple files at once, you'll see the same dialog. However, if you assign a set after the upload process is finished, you'll assign that set to all of the files. This is especially handy if you upload an entire gallery in one step. Just upload all of the files, assign the set with one action, and pull all of the files from that set into a slideshow.

Working with stacks

A **stack** is basically a collection of blocks you can reuse in multiple places on your site. Let's start by creating a new stack. You'll easily figure out the idea behind it with this little example! You can use the intelligent search bar at the top which you can focus by using the *Tab* key. Type stack and concrete5 will search for all of the choices containing the keyword stack:

Click on the first entry, **Stacks**. In the next screen, type the name of the new stack, for example, Contact Data in the **Name** field. Hit the **Add** button, click on the newly created stack, and you'll be forwarded to the following screen:

In this screen, you can add new blocks by clicking on the **Add Block** button. Adding new blocks works the same way as always from this point. Once you've added all of the blocks you want, you'll need to confirm the changes you've made to our stack by clicking on the **Approve Changes** button, seen here:

Click on the **Return to Website** link at the top-left corner to navigate back to your home page. Go to the page where you want to insert the Contact Data stack, click on the **Add To Sidebar** link, and select the **Add Stack** menu item, as shown in the following screenshot:

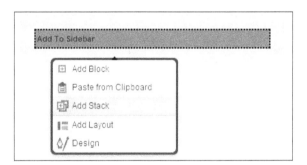

Select the **Contact Data** stack we created before and you'll see a new dialog. In this dialog, you either insert the entire stack with all of the blocks, or just a single block from the stack. This is, of course, only useful if you actually have more than one block in your stack. In our case, select the **Add Stack** menu item to insert the stack with all blocks.

If you click on the stack again, you'll see a menu which is slightly different from the menu you see when you click on a block. The first item is called **Manage Stack Contents** instead of edit. If you click on this item, you'll be redirected to the dashboard page where you've previously managed your stack. Here you can add, edit, or remove blocks, and once you approve the changes, the update is visible on all of the pages where this stack has been added.

If you need more detailed instructions, go to the following page and you'll see a video as well as some screenshots:

```
http://www.concrete5.org/documentation/using-concrete5/in-page-
editing/block-areas/stacks/
```

Change the layout and style of your pages, areas, and blocks

While most of your pages share the same logo as well as certain design elements, the content is quite likely to have a different structure. One page might have a sidebar, another page might have three columns, and another one might just have one big picture.

In concrete5, there are several ways to arrange your content in different structures. Each tool has certain advantages, and depending on your needs, you should pick the right one. We'll look at all of these tools in this section, making sure that at the end you'll know the right way to build the page structure you want.

Page types

Every page must have one and only one page type, never two or more than that. A page type is used in different ways. There are two applications for page types:

- A page type is a logical entity which you can use to build lists. Imagine you have a type called news. If you place a page list block in an area, you can build a list of all pages of that type and you'll have a news list. You can also use them to build something less obvious. In case you have your own car collection, create a page type car, insert a picture and some text to these pages, and you'll have a nice showcase to present your wealth or collection of toy cars.

- It's not a must, but most page types have a theme template as well. You can define a certain HTML structure and use it for a page type. This makes it easy to define the most-used layouts, such as a two-column and three-column layout.

Let's have a look at the pretty much self-explanatory screen where you can select the page types. You can open it by hovering over the **Edit** button in the concrete5 toolbar and clicking on the **Design** link:

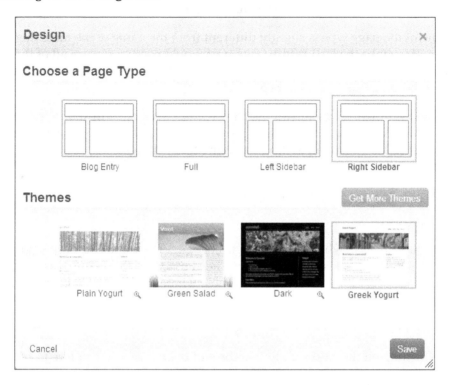

In the upper part of this screen, you can see all available types. Each type has a thumbnail assigned to it to give you an impression about the actual structure you're going to assign to your page. Select the one you need and confirm it by clicking on the **Save** button and you'll immediately see the new layout.

To get a better understanding of page types, look at the following block diagram:

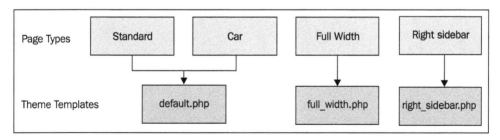

Every page type has an actual template, making sure the content is found in one or more containers. However, not every page type has its own template. As just mentioned, sometimes you just need a page type to make a group of certain pages and don't need a different HTML structure, and thus no PHP file.

The name of the page type is slightly different from the name of the matching template. If we take the **Full Width** page type, you'd need to replace all of the spaces with underscores, convert the text to lowercase, and append `.php`. The **Full Width** page type becomes `full_width.php`.

If there's no template that matches the page types, concrete5 will simply use `default.php` as a fallback. This is also why you should try to keep `default.php` as simple as possible and avoid adding too many fancy things.

Design to customize the appearance of blocks and areas

concrete5 has a feature which allows you to change some of the CSS properties without touching a single file. The design menu you need to see for this feature can be found in different places. There are three different places where this menu can be found:

- Clicking on an existing block
- Clicking on a stack you've inserted
- Clicking on the **Add to...** link at the end of an area while you're in edit mode

The screen you'll see is always the same, as shown in the following screenshot, but the element and the styles that are applied differ depending on the element where you've opened the design menu.

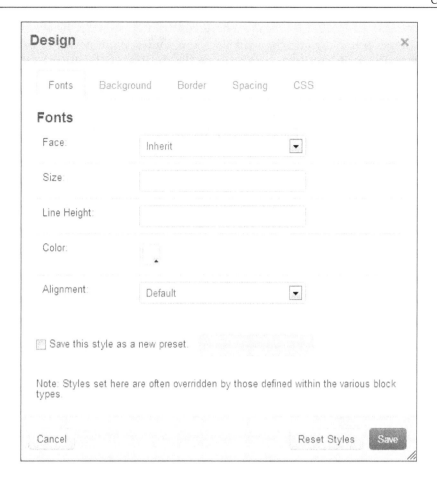

In this dialog, you can see a number of different properties. All of them are based on basic CSS rules with which you might be familiar. For those who want to go beyond the usual usage, there's a tab called **CSS** where you can enter your own CSS rules. Click on the **Save** button once you're done and the layout will change immediately.

Splitting content in different columns

Sometimes you might need a column structure different from anything you've seen available in the page types. You could create a new page type, but if it's a structure you just need once, it's probably better to use the layout feature. Let's have a look!

First, you need to navigate to the page where you want to split up the area. Change into the edit mode and click on the **Add To...** link underneath the area you want to split. Click on the **Add Layout** button and you'll see a dialog like this:

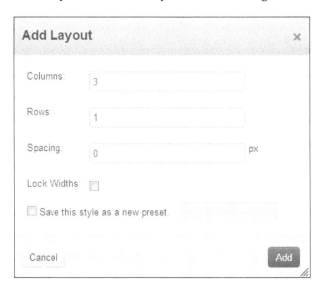

Specify the number of columns and rows you need as well as the spacing between the cells. You can later change the width of the columns by dragging handles above the area. If you want fixed widths, tick the **Lock Widths** checkbox. In case you want to use the same layout again, enable the last checkbox and enter a name. You can later select the previously created layouts again. After you've added the layout, you'll see more areas, as shown below:

The **Layout 1 : Cell 1** and **Layout 1: Cell 2** areas work like any other area, they are just half the size of the original **Main** area. Drag the handle in the middle to the left-hand side or to the right-hand side to change the column widths. The layout can be edited, removed, reordered, and locked by clicking on the plus icon at the top-left corner.

Creating and managing pages

While the default page structure is okay for a basic site, you'll probably want to have a different site structure. In concrete5, you can manage all of your pages in the in-site editing mode, but it's probably easier for most people if they have a hierarchical structure to look at.

Luckily, concrete5 offers this as well. Hover over the **Dashboard** button at the top and click on the **Full Sitemap** link in the little panel underneath the button. You'll be forwarded to a screen where you can see a common tree-like structure of all your pages, as shown in the following screenshot:

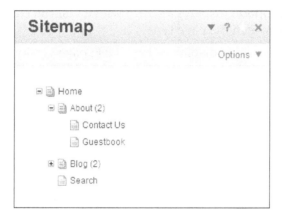

In this screen, you have all of the functions you'd expect from a tree-like structure. Each node with child elements can be expanded and collapsed. While this screen looks rather simple, there are a few hidden functions. Click on a node with your left mouse button and you should see a menu such as the one shown in the following screenshot:

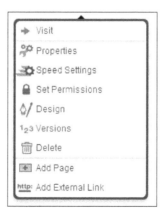

What's available here? The available options are explained as follows:

- **Visit**: This option opens the page in the current browser window.

- **Properties**: This option edits the page name, meta title, and any other attribute you've assigned to your pages.

- **Speed Settings**: This option shows the various caching options to improve the performance of your site. There's usually no need to worry about it unless you have a big site.

- **Set Permissions**: This option shows different options to hide a page from certain groups.

- **Design**: This option displays a screen where you can change the page theme for a page or switch the page type.

- **Versions**: This option displays all available page versions. It also offers the option to undo a change by reapproving an old version.

- **Delete**: Tired of that page? Remove it with this function. You can restore pages that you've accidentally deleted in the site map. Display system pages there and you'll find an item called trash where you'll find the deleted pages.

- **Add Page**: This option allows you to add a new subpage underneath the one you've selected.

- **Add External Link**: The site structure you build in the sitemap is directly used to build the navigation. This is the reason why you do not only add pages to the tree, but also external links. Want to open `http://www.concrete5.org/` from your sites navigation? Add an external link!

Adding a new page

Let's have a look at the process for adding a new page to your site. If you're not already in the site map, hover over the **Dashboard** button at the top and click on the **Full Sitemap** link.

Click on the page underneath where you'd like to have a new page. In this example, we want to create a new page showing the location of our office:

In the first step, you need to select the page type you want to use as the new page (as shown below). Your choice doesn't really matter much and you can change it at any time if you are not content with your decision:

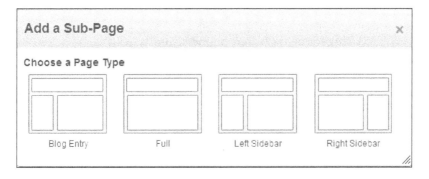

Before the page is created, there's one more step where you need to enter at least the name of the new page:

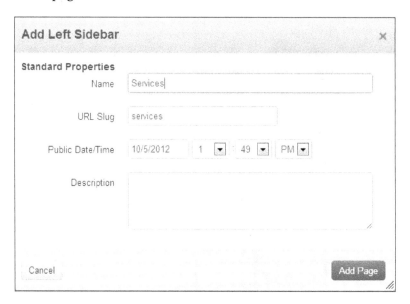

The **URL Slug** field is automatically updated while you're entering the name. The value in this field is shown in the URL of your new page. If you're creating a new page about the services you offer, as shown in the preceding screenshot, the URL will look like this:

```
http://www.your-site.com/services/
```

URL slug for better search engine visibility

Search engines scan the URL of your pages as well as the content. Having the right keyword in the URL is one of the many indicators for search engines that make your pages relevant for that keyword.

If you're testing cars, you better use a **URL slug** such as `car-testing-services` instead of `services`.

The **Public/Date Time** field is only informative by default, but can be used in custom blocks to sort or filter pages. We don't need that part and use the default value.

If you create a list of pages by using the `Page List` block, you'll see a link to the page as well as a description, if available. The description shown in the page list block is pulled from the **Description** field. Enter a summary of your page if you intend to show it in a list, for example, a news list.

Adding default blocks to page types

When you create a new page, there's usually not much in it. Depending on the theme, you'll only see the logo and maybe some information in the footer. It is sometimes helpful if there's some default content in a new page. Imagine if your site has a header picture in every page, wouldn't it be nice if there was a default picture for new pages?

Hit the *Tab* key to focus the intelligent search bar at the top and enter `page types`. Select the first item and you'll see a screen similar to the following screenshot:

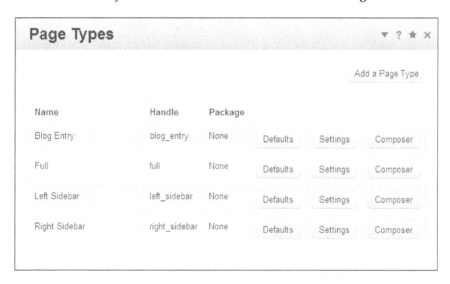

Click on the **Defaults** button and you'll see a screen much like the edit mode of a page we worked with before. Everything works like on a normal page, but the blocks you add here will show up when you create a new page of that type. More about this feature can be found at the following location:

```
http://www.concrete5.org/documentation/using-concrete5/dashboard/
pages-and-themes/page-types/defaults/
```

Summary

In this chapter, we had a quick look at the different features in concrete5 to get familiar with editing content. Take your time with this chapter as it's important that you understand how you can edit content and work with page types before you continue with the next chapter.

If the instructions in this chapter were too short, the official concrete5 site has some more detailed tutorials as well as videos. Check out the following link if you need more information:

`http://www.concrete5.org/documentation/using-concrete5/`

2
Architecture of concrete5

We've looked at the basic operations in concrete5 in *Chapter 1, Getting Started*. You should now be familiar with using concrete5 and be able to update most of the content. Before we start building our own theme, we're going to dig into a few things in the background of concrete5.

This chapter is not a must, and if you're not eager to understand the technical things in the background, feel free to skip it. However, if you plan on using concrete5 for more than just one personal site, read this chapter to get a better understanding of the inner workings of concrete5. This should also help you if a customer of yours wants to know what's possible with concrete5. Knowing what can be done out of the box can help a graphic designer as well, even if he's not going to write the code himself.

You'll see that while you're building your own theme, you'll slowly start to understand a few pieces of concrete5. If you read this chapter, you should be able to connect these pieces a bit quicker, and you'll soon be a master of concrete5.

The file structure of concrete5

One important thing to remember when working with concrete5 is not to change any files underneath the `concrete` and `updates` directory! Let's have a closer look at the reasons with the help of the following screenshot:

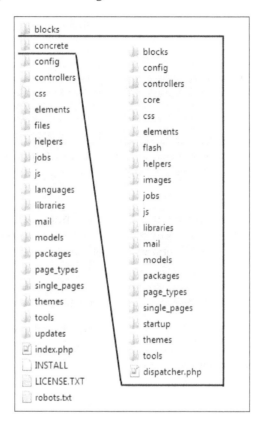

As you can see, there are quite a few directories if you install concrete5, but don't worry about that, you'll just need a few of them.

Why is the `concrete` directory sacred? If you look at the previous screenshot, you can see that the `concrete` directory contains more or less the same directories like you have in the root. That's mostly because concrete5 uses the same framework for its backend and editing system as you're using to build your own websites and applications. In other words, the actual CMS code can be found in the `concrete` directory, and whatever you build is outside in the other top-level directories.

Here's a list of the most-used directories and their purposes:

- `blocks`: This includes the block you build for your own site and when you want to add templates for existing blocks.
- `concrete`: As previously mentioned, this is the core of the CMS. Don't touch any files in this directory!
- `config`: There's one important file in this directory, `site.php`, where you'll find some of your settings such as the credentials to access the database.
- `files`: If you upload files by using the concrete5 file manager, you'll fill this directory. You can also find some cache related files such as thumbnails in this directory. There's hardly ever a reason to manually change something in this directory.
- `languages`: You'll need to upload language files in this directory if you want to use concrete5 in a different language. Check this page for more details:

  `http://www.concrete5.org/developers/translate/`

- `packages`: When you build your own packages, you'll need to save them in this directory. Also, when you install an add-on from the marketplace, you'll find its code in this directory.
- `themes`: This is the directory you'll need if you want to customize the appearance of your site.
- `updates`: This is where you'll find newer versions of the core if you update them through the dashboard.

concrete5 updates

As with most software, concrete5 gets some updates from time to time. If you look at the official code repository at `https://github.com/concrete5/concrete5/`, you'll see that there are plenty of code changes. Sometimes it's about bug fixing, but often you'll also see new features being added to the core.

Before we update concrete5, you might want to create a database backup. Follow these steps to do so:

1. Enter `Backup` in the intelligent search box in the top-right corner and select the first entry.
2. Click on **Run Backup** to create the database backup.

Let's have a look at the process of updating concrete5:

1. Hit *Tab* to focus the intelligent search box in the top-right corner.
2. Enter Update concrete5 and select the only item in the result.
3. You'll either get a message telling you that there are no updates available or a screen like this:

As mentioned in the screenshot, clicking on the **Download** button doesn't install anything. It will simply download the new core. If you want to update your site, you'll need to confirm the update in another screen which appears after you've downloaded the new core.

After you've confirmed the update process in the second screen, you'll immediately have an up-to-date concrete5 site. But what did happen in the background? The update process did not overwrite the existing core but rather added a new core. If you check the previously mentioned updates directory, you'll notice that there's a new sub-directory, as shown in the following screenshot:

But how does concrete5 know where to look for the new core? You can probably figure out the answer on your own if you have a look at the content of `config/site.php`:

```
define('DB_SERVER', 'localhost');
define('DB_USERNAME', 'c5book');
define('DB_PASSWORD', 'wlx..2AAdapp');
define('DB_DATABASE', 'c5book');
define('PASSWORD_SALT', 'nESkwx4K8g8Lnh5YI4');
define('DIRNAME_APP_UPDATED', 'concrete5.6.0.2');
```

The last line tells concrete5 that the currently active core is located in `updates/concrete5.6.0.2`. What's nice about this is the fact that you can simply remove that line and it will go back to the original core or change the version number and it will point to another core located in the `updates` directory. But don't forget, you cannot go back to a previous version without taking care of the database. With probably every new concrete5 version there are changes in the database structure which aren't backwards compatible. Make sure you restore the correct database backup before switching back to an older core!

Caching for better performance

concrete5 ships with a caching functionality which improves the performance of certain elements. However, when you work on your new site, you'll often modify a number of files. Imagine what happens with a cache if you do that. A caching function has some difficulties in knowing that it has to invalidate its content and render the output again. It's not a big deal but it can be annoying. Luckily, it's easy to avoid.

When you build a new site, you might want to consider disabling all of the caches and enabling them again once you've finished the site. Type `cache` in the intelligent search box and select **Cache & Speed Settings**. You'll see a screen with a few radio buttons you can switch to *Off*. After you save the changes, your site won't use the cache anymore and won't bother you while you work on your files. Depending on your server and site, the cache might not give you any benefit or even run slower, but if it does, make sure you enable it again before you show your new site to the public.

The distinction of Model-View-Controller (MVC)

When working with concrete5 blocks and single pages, you'll come in contact with a pattern called MVC. It's short for Model-View-Controller and is one of the most-used patterns in software design.

It tries to make sure that the code stays clean, has a structure which is easy to understand, and keeps the application stable. It achieves this by splitting the code into different parts. Let's have a look at the following diagram:

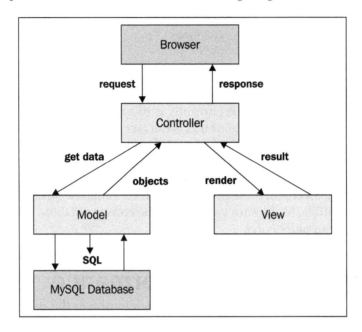

We've added two elements, **Browser** and **MySQL Database**, which don't belong to the actual pattern. They are just included to make it easier for you to understand how this pattern works. You can see that if you request a page, it will be forwarded to **Controller**. The validation of the data should be a part of **Model,** and **View** contains the actual output template. **Controller** knows how to handle all of these parts. It's the element that connects most of the things.

If there is any persistent data involved, you'll quite likely have a model as well. A model is basically a layer you add before accessing the database. Why add this overhead? A model has several benefits:

- If you change your database, there's just one place where you need to check and fix your code, that is, the model.

- Got any performance issues with your database? Look in the model and you'll find everything you need to tune.

- Want to add an attribute *deleted* to mark a table record as deleted instead of actually removing it? If you have a model for that table type, there's just one file where you need to make that change in. There is no need to search for the name of the table in your entire project.

At the end, it's also nice because if you structure your code this way, it's also easy to understand for a lot of people. This improves the maintainability and the chances that someone else wants to work with your code.

The last element is pretty obvious, it's called view and does the actual rendering of your output. It's the place where most HTML markup can be found.

The MVC pattern won't be used when you build your first theme, but as soon as you start to change the design of the built-in login page, you'll see a part of that pattern. Understanding it helps you to avoid looking in the wrong place and also allows you to dig a bit deeper into the code.

The anatomy of a page

Every page belonging to a theme has a certain structure. You can use a different structure, but you should probably keep using the one used by the core and almost every marketplace theme. Let's have a look at three different files from a theme. We'll create them on our own in the next chapter. For now, we're just looking at them to help you with reading the code.

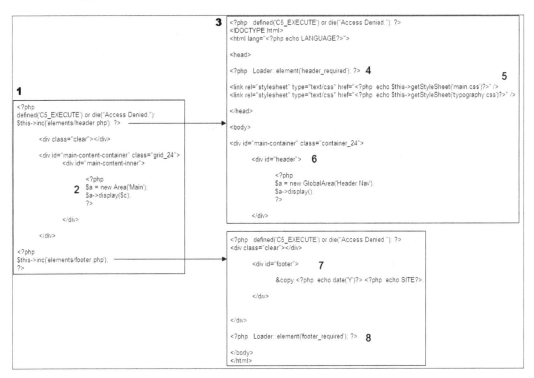

There are several numbers shown in the previous illustration, let's have a quick look at them:

1. This is the page theme template, for example, `full.php` or `default.php`. It's the file rendered by concrete5, and therefore the one holding everything from the theme together.

2. Each theme template can have a different HTML structure, one might have a single column, another one two and maybe even some dynamic code. In our case, we simple have one content and one area where the user can insert blocks.

3. This file is called `header.php` and is located in the `elements` directory of the theme. It's included by the theme template and usually shared by all page type templates.

4. This line is mandatory. As concrete5 uses an inline editing system, it has to find a way to inject its code into your theme. This line also makes sure that meta tags managed by concrete5 appear on your site.

5. If you have any additional elements such as a JavaScript or CSS file, place it here.

6. The header can contain an area as well, but keep in mind that this area will be visible in every page type. A common usage for this is the `Header Nav` area where you can insert the navigation.

7. This file is called `footer.php` and is also located in the `elements` directory. You can insert anything you want to display at the bottom of each page.

8. This is another part where concrete5 can inject JavaScript, tracking codes, and similar things into your page. It's mandatory as well.

This illustration should have given you a quick overview, but don't worry, we'll have another look at this in more detail when we build our own theme.

The anatomy of a block

We won't go into the details of building a new block, if you want to go beyond themes, have a look at the book *concrete5 Beginner's Guide, Packt Publishing* or read the following tutorial:

```
http://www.concrete5.org/documentation/developers/blocks/
understanding-and-building-blocks-in-concrete5
```

The only thing we want to know is where a block can be found and what kind of files you'll usually find there. This knowledge can be helpful, even if you just want to customize the layout. Parts of the layout in your site are, of course, generated by the theme, but there are also parts which are created by different blocks. While an HTML editor block doesn't do much more than printing the text you've entered, there are blocks (such as the form block) where you have a more complex output, which might need a bit of styling.

There are four different places where you can find blocks:

- /blocks/: This is for blocks in the root of your website. This directory is empty unless you add your own blocks there.

- /packages/<package-name>/blocks/: This is for blocks which are part of packages. This directory is also empty unless you installed new packages or created a package yourself.

- /concrete/blocks/: This is where you can find the core blocks.

- /updates/<concrete-version>/blocks/: This is where you can find the core blocks in case you've updated your concrete5 installation.

Let's start by looking at the YouTube block included in the default installation of concrete5. All of the files of this block are found in /concrete/blocks/youtube/, and are shown below:

This block is a nice example to start with, as it only contains those files which are really required.

- add.php: This file is included when you add a new instance of a block. It often includes form_setup_html.php.

- controller.php: As the name suggests, this file is responsible for the control of the block, saving data, preparing the output, etc. It's basically where all of the logical operations happen.

- db.xml: Most blocks need persistent data, and this is where you specify the table and column structure used by a block.

- `edit.php`: This file is included when you edit an existing instance of a block. It often includes `form_setup_html.php`.

- `form_setup_html.php`: This is a common file shared by `add.php` and `edit. php` in case the form to manage the block works the same way when adding and editing a block.

- `icon.png`: This is a 16 x 16 pixel icon which is shown when you select the block from the list of available blocks.

- `view.php`: This file is responsible for creating the HTML markup visible to the site visitors.

XML database table definition

If you want to know more about the XML used to define the database structure, check the following page for more background information:

`http://phplens.com/lens/adodb/docs-datadict.htm`

Using this XML makes it easier for you to change the database structure in the future. No need to write *alter* statements, changes to the XML structure are automatically applied without removing the existing data.

concrete5 API and helpers

concrete5 is mostly a CMS, but also a framework. Some parts have been borrowed from Zend framework but a lot of code is concrete5-specific. That's mostly because concrete5 has a longer history than most people think.

But despite its history, building applications, and not just simple websites, is a joy and not complicated at all. It might take some time until you understand the most important classes and libraries, but it's definitely worth the effort.

We won't cover all of the different helpers, libraries, and models, we're just going to look at some major elements to give you a quick overview. It should be enough to get you started if you ever want to dive deeper into concrete5.

Helpers

If you look at the directory `/concrete/helpers`, you'll find a number of files supposed to make your life easier. There are helpers to work with dates, JSON objects, pagination, form items, validation, text sanitation, and of course a number of helpers rather specific for concrete5 items.

The official online documentation has a more detailed explanation of these helpers, so have a look at this page if you want to work with forms:

```
http://www.concrete5.org/documentation/developers/helpers/core-user-
interface/
```

Or:

```
http://www.concrete5.org/documentation/developers/forms/standard-
widgets/
```

To give you an impression about helpers, the following code snippet is one short example that sends a plain e-mail:

```php
<?php
$mh = Loader::helper('mail');
$mh->setSubject('Hello lovely World');
$mh->setBody('Have a great day!');
$mh->to('the@world.org', 'The World');
$mh->from('me@switzerland.ch');
$mh->sendMail();
```

It starts with the loader specific to concrete5. It's what you'll need to load all kinds of objects, whether a library, model, helper, etc. All other lines are self-explanatory.

You might wonder why you should use this helper and not just go with the PHP function mail. After all, more people will know about the mail function. There are several reasons for this:

- The concrete5 mail helper makes certain tasks much easier. Working with HTML mails, as well as mail templates, is done with just a few lines of code. There is no need to reinvent the wheel on top of mail.

- When you use the mail helper, you'll automatically see your mail in the log available in the dashboard. If you worked with Internet projects before, you'll probably have had a customer complaining that he didn't get the mail from the contact form on his site. With concrete5, you just need to look into the log and have the answer you're looking for.

- If you're working on a site, you want to make sure your customers aren't bothered with a ton of test mails. If you use the mail helper, you can set a constant called ENABLE_EMAILS to false in config/site.php and it won't deliver any messages. Once you're done, remove that constant or set it to true and you're ready to go.

The mail helper is just one of many examples where concrete5 can help you to be more productive and often faster when developing new applications.

Events to hook into the core

Without going into any technical details, concrete5 raises a number of different events with which your own add-ons can interact. If you want to synchronize the users created, modified, and removed in concrete5 with your own system, hook into these events and you can run your own code whenever someone changes something related to users.

These events can be related to the following elements:

- **Pages**: To interact when a new page is created, removed, approved, and so on.
- **Users and groups**: To run custom code upon changes happening to these objects.
- **Files**: To execute your own code when someone uploads, edits, removes a file, and so on.

You can find the complete list of events on the following page:

`http://www.concrete5.org/documentation/developers/system/events`

If you build your own add-ons, you can also dispatch your own events. You're not restricted to the default events.

What happens when a page is rendered

Unlike a site with static HTML files, the content in concrete5 is stored in a database. If you view a page, all of that content needs to find its way to the visitor's browser. Working with FTP is not going to work anymore and might be a bit unusual for those who haven't worked with a database-based CMS before.

To give you a rough overview about what actually happens when a page is viewed, here's the summarized flow when a page is requested:

1. The visitor requests a page such as `http://www.your-site.com/about/`.
2. Apache gets a request, and assuming that you've enabled pretty URLs, it will parse a file called `.htaccess` in the root of your site. Here's a part of its content:

```
RewriteEngine On
RewriteBase /
RewriteCond %{REQUEST_FILENAME} !-f
RewriteCond %{REQUEST_FILENAME}/index.html !-f
RewriteCond %{REQUEST_FILENAME}/index.php !-f
RewriteRule . index.php [L]
```

3. REQUEST_FILENAME contains the file that the user requested. -f means that we only executed the RewriteRule if the file doesn't actually exist. As /about doesn't actually exist, it won't stop the execution. Instead, it will run into RewriteRule and forward the request to index.php. In other words, if the page you request doesn't exist as a file, it will be forwarded to index.php.

4. What happens in index.php? If you look at the content, you'll see that it only includes concrete/dispatcher.php.

5. The dispatcher contains quite a lot of code. We won't cover everything, just a few of the more important things that happen:

   ° Activate the proper error handling
   ° Read the configuration files
   ° Load the database
   ° Create the sessions
   ° Check and process the localization settings
   ° Check for events that need to be executed
   ° Parse the URL to get the page object that has to be rendered
   ° Render the view of the page object and process all of the blocks in the page

You can find a bit more about the dispatcher on the following page:

http://www.concrete5.org/documentation/introduction/dispatcher-and-application-flow/

Why you might want to build a package

In concrete5, you can build all of the objects used in the CMS yourself. No matter if it's a block, a theme, a maintenance task, or a custom attribute, there are APIs for everything and you don't need to touch the core code of the CMS. But imagine if you have a huge project where you build some blocks as well as some jobs. If you just read the previous paragraphs, you might think that you need to put all of the elements in the top-level folders: blocks and jobs. This is where a package can be handy.

Before we have a closer look at the packages, here's what a package offers you:

* The ability to wrap several things such as blocks, jobs, and attributes in one directory.

- An installer you can use to check requirements, add default configurations, create database tables, install new attributes, add default data, add new blocks or themes, and basically manage everything your packages needs to work.

- A package can be submitted and sold on the official `concrete5.org` marketplace.

Basic package installer

As this book is about building themes, let's have a look at the basic package installer you will need if you want to put your theme into a package. It's basically everything you need if you want to sell your theme at the marketplace to make some money.

Every package needs its own directory. Therefore, create a directory called `theme_book` in the top-level directory `packages`. Within that directory, create a file called `controller.php`. The structure at this moment should look as shown in the following screenshot:

Open `controller.php` and put the following content in it:

```php
<?php
defined('C5_EXECUTE') or die('Access Denied.');

class ThemeBookPackage extends Package {

    protected $pkgHandle = 'theme_book';
```

```
    protected $appVersionRequired = '5.6.0';
    protected $pkgVersion = '1.0';

    public function getPackageDescription() {
        return t("Installs the Book theme.");
    }

    public function getPackageName() {
        return t("Book Theme");
    }

    public function install() {
        $pkg = parent::install();
        PageTheme::add('theme_book', $pkg);
    }

}
```

It's important that you make sure the name of the directory matches the name of the controller. But take care, it's not exactly the same but follows a clear rule. The name of the class, ThemeBookPackage, is created by using the following rules, also called CamelCase:

- A capital letter at the beginning
- A capital letter after each underscore
- Underscores need to be removed
- The word Package has to be appended to the string

The value of $pkgHandle needs to match the package directory and theme_book in PageTheme::add('theme_book', $pkg); needs to match the name of the theme directory in themes. The name of the theme and the package is usually the same!

It's not necessary in order to get your package installer working, but if you want to submit your package to the marketplace, you'll need to add a package icon as well. This is a pretty easy task, just create a picture with the dimensions 97 x 97 pixels and make sure you have a rounded corner of four pixels. Save that picture in the same directory where controller.php is located, under the name icon.png.

Downloading the example code

You can download the example code files for all Packt books you have purchased from your account at http://www.PacktPub.com. If you purchased this book elsewhere, you can visit http://www.PacktPub.com/support and register to have the files e-mailed directly to you.

Once you've finished the next chapter, you can try to place all of your theme files in the `themes` folder from the package, go to your site, hit *Tab* to focus the intelligent search bar, enter `add functionality`, and then click on **Install**, as seen below:

Please note that you need to activate the theme after you've installed the package. You can get to the screen where you can activate an installed theme if you type `themes` in the intelligent search box in the top-right corner.

Marketplace submission

Wrapping your theme in a package is the first step if you want to publish your work on the marketplace, but it's not the only thing you need to do. Here's a summary of the most important rules you need to follow:

- It's wrapped in a package and installs and uninstalls without any problems,
- You must have privileges to the code as well as all of the assets used in your theme.
- There needs to be an icon with 4-pixel rounded corners with a width and height of 97 pixels.
- You need to give support in case a customer can't install your theme or has another problem with it.

There are quite a few more rules, most of them are easy to understand, but make sure you check the following official page as well:

`http://www.concrete5.org/developers/marketplace-submission-rules/`

At the end of the page is a link where you can get to the form allowing you to submit your add-on.

Summary

In this chapter, we looked at a lot of different technical things in concrete5. By now, you should have a first impression about the architecture of concrete5 as well as an understanding of what's possible with concrete5.

You probably aren't an expert in concrete5 development yet, at least not if you only read this chapter and haven't worked with concrete5 before, but you should know some of the relevant keywords in concrete5 and be able to start digging in if you need to.

Don't worry if you didn't understand every part in this chapter, it's just meant to give you a head start if you want to go beyond the creation of themes.

3
Creating Your First Theme

If you got to this point, you should have a basic understanding about concrete5. We haven't done any coding so far, but you should be familiar with concrete5 from the user's side and have some rough knowledge about its possible uses.

In this chapter we'll start creating our own files. You'll need access to a site where you can modify and create files (it's not just about modifying files). It doesn't matter if this site runs on a remote server or on your local computer. Whatever suits you is okay.

You'll also need a text editor such as Notepad++ or a complete IDE such as NetBeans to work with your PHP, CSS, and JS files, as well as a tool such as FileZilla to upload your files if you're working on a remote server.

At the end of this chapter, you'll have a basic theme of your own. It's not going to be fancy, but you should have the understanding you need to make changes on your own by using your CSS and HTML knowledge.

Getting started with themes

The first example we're going to create will be a rather simple theme without a lot of HTML or CSS code. It's just an example to show you the most important elements in a concrete5 theme. In order to keep things simple, we'll use the Bootstrap library created by Twitter.

Bootstrap is a frontend framework that can often help you to be faster and more efficient when creating websites and applications. There are a bunch of CSS classes you can use to get better looking elements than plain HTML would produce, but it also comes with several JavaScript functions such as a carousel gallery, a drop-down navigation, and a few more. If you haven't heard of it before, you should probably have a look at their site to get a first impression about it:

```
http://twitter.github.com/bootstrap/
```

Creating the first theme

Let's start by creating the directory structure we need for our theme. Look for the `themes` directory in the root of your concrete5 site and create a new directory called `bootstrap1`. We're going to create several versions, thus the number at the end.

Within that directory, create two more directories called `css` and `elements`. Download the Bootstrap framework, (there's a big download button when you navigate to `http://twitter.github.com/bootstrap/`) and extract the files into a temporary directory. We only need one file at this point; it's called `bootstrap.min.css` and can be found in the `css` directory. Copy that file into our theme's `css` directory.

The structure should now look like the following screenshot:

Every theme has to have a name and a short description. For this, create a new file in `bootstrap1` called `description.txt` and insert two lines. The first is the name and the second is the description. Following is an example, but feel free to use whatever you like:

```
bootstrap theme #1
book demo theme by Remo Laubacher
```

Your theme's directory structure should now look like the following screenshot:

Adding our page type template

Now we're going to add the actual theme code, that is, the HTML code along with some very basic PHP snippets. If you still remember what you read in *Chapter 1, Getting Started*, you should know that you can have several page types, each with the possibility of having a different layout. But as the page types can also be used as logical elements to group and combine things, it's not necessary to have a different layout for each type.

That's why there's always a default layout that is used if the page type doesn't need a specific layout. The file used for those types is called `default.php` and has to be located in the root of your theme where you just created the file to hold the description of our theme. You might want to have another look at the graphic shown in *Chapter 2, Architecture of concrete5*, about the anatomy of a page. It should give you the bigger picture that you need to understand how each of these elements come together. After that, create the `default.php` file and put the following content in it:

```php
<?php defined('C5_EXECUTE') or die('Access Denied.') ?>

<?php
$this->inc('elements/header.php');
?>

<div class="row-fluid">
    <div class="span9">
            <?php
            $areaMain = new Area('Main');
            $areaMain->display($c);
            ?>
    </div>
    <div class="span3">
        <div class="well sidebar-nav">
            <?php
            $areaSidebar = new Area('Sidebar');
            $areaSidebar->display($c);
            ?>
        </div>
    </div>
</div>

<?php
$this->inc('elements/footer.php');
?>
```

It's simple but let's still have a closer look at it; it's important that you completely understand what happens here. We will see the following elements in the code:

- `defined('C5_EXECUTE') or die('Access Denied.')`: Every request to a PHP file should be handled by the concrete5 framework and therefore gets routed through `index.php`. This line makes sure that a direct call to our PHP file isn't possible. By doing this, we can make sure the code is always used in the way it's meant and doesn't throw any errors, or even worse, opens a security hole.

- `$this->inc('elements/header.php')`: This is basically just an include that pulls the content of another file, in this case `header.php`, in the `elements` directory. Its basic usage is to avoid redundant code once we add more files to our theme. It also helps you to keep your theme clean and tidy. By the way, the same goes for the footer. If you have another element that you might want to share across different files, feel free to add as many elements and includes as you want.

- `$areaMain = new Area('Main')`: In concrete5, you place your content (blocks) in areas. This code adds a new area with the name specified in the brackets to your theme. There's always a second command you have to use, to actually display the area: `$areaMain->display($c);`. This command takes the newly created `area` object and prints it to the collection object `$c`. The variable `$c` is set by concrete5 and refers to the current page. If you go beyond themes and start diving into the concrete5 core, you'll be able to use this fact to display areas and their blocks from different pages. You can easily create a mess with this, but on the other hand, you can also avoid some redundancy. For now let's keep using `$c` — it's what you'll need in 99 percent of all cases.

Global variables

As you've seen, we're using a global variable called `$c` to get a reference to the current page. This is an often used variable; but as global variables are frequently considered bad (after all you can't really see where `$c` is coming from without reading a lot of code.) you might want to use `Page::getCurrentPage()`. You can either use it directly, for example `$areaMain->display(Page::getCurrentPage());`, or assign it to `$c` with `$c = Page::getCurrentPage()` and then keep using `$c`.

Creating the shared header

We've already included two files, `header.php` and `footer.php` but haven't created them yet. In the `elements` directory, create these two files. Your structure should look like the following screenshot; it's also everything we need to use our theme:

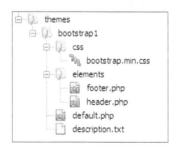

The following code belongs to the header. If you already have your own HTML code, this is more or less the beginning of it with some PHP commands. If you want, you can already try to use your own HTML code, but if you don't feel confident enough, take the following example code to continue:

```php
<?php defined('C5_EXECUTE') or die('Access Denied.') ?>
<!DOCTYPE html>
<html lang="en">
    <head>
        <link rel="stylesheet" media="screen" type="text/css"
href="<?php echo $this->getThemePath() ?>/css/bootstrap.min.css" />

        <!--HTML5 shim, for IE6-8 support of HTML5 elements -->
        <!--[if lt IE 9]>
          <script src="http://html5shim.googlecode.com/svn/trunk/
html5.js"></script>
        <![endif]-->

        <?php Loader::element('header_required') ?>
    </head>

    <body>

        <div id="wrapper">
            <nav class="navbar">
                <div class="navbar-inner">
                <?php
                $areaNav = new Area('Header Nav');
                $areaNav->display($c);
                ?>
                </div>
            </nav>
        </div>

        <div class="container-fluid">
```

Again, let's have a closer look at this code:

- `<?php echo $this->getThemePath() ?>/css/bootstrap.min.css`: We're using getThemePath to get the current path to our theme and append the file we want to include. Using getThemePath makes sure that the file can be found, even if you install concrete5 in a subdirectory.

- `<script src="http://html5shim.googlecode.com/svn/trunk/html5.js"></script>`: You might have noticed the DOCTYPE that tells the browser that we're using HTML5. Old versions of Internet Explorer aren't able to handle the new tags unless you use some JavaScript to fix that issue. This is done by using the html5shiv library. More information about this can be found at `http://code.google.com/p/html5shiv/`.

- `<?php Loader::element('header_required') ?>`: This is specific to concrete5. Elements such as meta tags are managed in concrete5 and therefore saved in the database. Adding this nifty snippet makes sure that concrete5 is able to add that information as well as some JavaScripts that add-ons want to add to your site. The `Loader` class is a class you'll often use when you want to access concrete5 resources such as libraries, helpers, models, and in this case an element. `header_required` is a file and a part of the core you can find in `concrete/elements/header_required.php`.

Creating the shared footer

The `footer.php` file is a bit simpler than the header. Insert the following lines and you're done:

```php
<?php defined('C5_EXECUTE') or die('Access Denied.') ?>

<footer>
    <p>&copy; <?php echo SITE . ' ' . date('Y') ?></p>
</footer>

</div>
<?php Loader::element('footer_required') ?>

</body>
</html>
```

Let's have a look at the two lines in the footer:

- `<?php echo SITE . ' ' . date('Y') ?>`: Sites where the copyright ended a few years ago are pretty common. It's easy to forget that date at the bottom of every page. Set it right by making it dynamic using `date('Y')` and you don't have to worry about it. We also use the `SITE` constant, which pulls the name of the site you entered during the installation. This makes sure that you can use your theme for different sites and don't have to change anything.

- `<?php Loader::element('footer_required') ?>`: This is very similar to the previously mentioned `<?php Loader::element('header_required') ?>` element, where we've included a file called `header_required`, but this time it's the footer where you'll find items added by add-ons too. If you wonder what exactly happens here, have a look at `concrete/elements/footer_required.php`.

Adding a theme thumbnail

Thumbnail is not necessary for this example but it looks odd when you install your theme and there's just a plain white rectangle, and the themes you want to submit to the marketplace need it. Every theme should have a thumbnail with the dimension of 120 x 90 pixels saved as `thumbnail.png`.

After you created and saved that picture, the final structure of your theme should look like the following screenshot:

Installing your theme

Now that we have all the necessary items in our theme including a thumbnail, we're ready to install it. Focus on the intelligent search box at the top, enter `themes`, and select the first entry. At the top you'll see all the installed themes; at the bottom you can find our new theme:

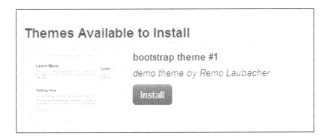

After you've installed the theme, you can activate it. As we haven't added any CSS files yet, it will look rather ugly, but feel free to activate it and have a look at it; you can always go back and activate another theme. It might help you if you first activate the theme and reload your page a few times while we add more files to it; you'll see how the different files come together.

Adding CSS files to a theme

There's just one CSS file in our theme so far and it's not even one that we've created on our own. You probably want to add some of your own CSS as well to make your site look a bit more tailor-made.

Most themes have two additional CSS files, one called `main.css` and the other called `typography.css`. Let's start with the first one.

Adding main.css

We start by creating a clone of our previous theme `bootstrap1` called `bootstrap2`.

Create a new file called `main.css` in the root of your theme. This file is going to contain all the CSS rules that you need to implement in your layout. Feel free to add anything you like; here's just one small suggestion—the current layout will take all the space it gets, which makes it look rather big if you have a big screen. Adding the following content to your new CSS file will change that:

```css
.container-fluid {
    max-width: 970px;
}
```

You have to insert the highlighted line shown as follows, into your `header.php`, which is located in the elements directory of your theme:

```php
<?php defined('C5_EXECUTE') or die('Access Denied.') ?>

<!DOCTYPE html>
<html lang="en">
    <head>
        <link rel="stylesheet" media="screen" type="text/css"
href="<?php echo $this->getThemePath() ?>/css/bootstrap.min.css" />
        <link rel="stylesheet" media="screen" type="text/css"
href="<?php echo $this->getStylesheet('main.css') ?>" />

            <!--[if lt IE 9]>
```

```
        <script src="http://html5shim.googlecode.com/svn/trunk/
html5.js"></script>
        <![endif]-->

        <?php Loader::element('header_required'); ?>

    </head>
```

Using a wrapper class

The concrete5 edit toolbar is embedded in your website if you're logged in. As you can probably imagine, this might cause some issues if your theme changes some elements globally. Adding a { color: white; } can cause all links to be white, even those in the concrete5 toolbar.

An easy trick to fix this is to wrap your markup with a div element having an ID like page; for example, <div id="page">. You can then use this to limit the scope of your styles by using #page a { color: white; } instead of a { color: white; }.

Adding typography.css

We've already added a custom CSS file; you might wonder why we want to add another one. You're certainly entitled to ask that question; adding a second resource without any benefit should be avoided, after all.

However, the typography.css file has one feature which might prompt you to create this additional file. When you enter formatted text using the content block, you can already see some formatted text; it has a certain size, color, and more. Wouldn't it be nice if the content block would already show you the correct font color, styles, and so on?

That's why you need the typography file!

The CSS file is loaded in the content block as well. To check this out, we're going to add a file called typography.css in our current theme bootstrap2. We're going to use it to make the black color of our headings a bit lighter by inserting the following content:

```
h1, h2, h3, h4, h5, h6 {
    color: #555;
}
```

We have to include this new file in our theme to make sure it's also used when viewing the page. To do this, open the header.php file in your theme's elements directory. You'll have to insert a new line, but note that the following snippet doesn't show you the complete code you have in header.php; just make sure you insert the highlighted line:

```php
<?php defined('C5_EXECUTE') or die('Access Denied.') ?>

<!DOCTYPE html>
<html lang="en">
    <head>
        <link rel="stylesheet" media="screen" type="text/css"
href="<?php echo $this->getThemePath() ?>/css/bootstrap.min.css" />
        <link rel="stylesheet" media="screen" type="text/css"
href="<?php echo $this->getStylesheet('main.css') ?>" />
        <link rel="stylesheet" media="screen" type="text/css"
href="<?php echo $this->getThemePath() ?>/typography.css" />

        <!-- Le HTML5 shim, for IE6-8 support of HTML5 elements -->
        <!--[if lt IE 9]>
          <script src="http://html5shim.googlecode.com/svn/trunk/
html5.js"></script>
        <![endif]-->

        <?php Loader::element('header_required'); ?>

    </head>
```

Once you've added this file, you can go ahead and edit a page of your choice. If you open the content block, you'll notice that the headings have a slightly brighter color. For those in need of a better pair of eyes, replace #555 with red and you should see the change as well. It might happen that you don't see the changes immediately because of caching issues. If that happens, clear your browser's cache and reload the page.

Content block styles

Let's have a look at another quick CSS thing you can do with the content block of concrete5. If you had a closer look at the content block, you might have seen that there's an empty drop-down menu called **Styles**. It's very useful to us this way and only takes a short time to change.

If you already closed it, open typography.css again and make sure it looks like the following code:

```
h1, h2, h3, h4, h5, h6 {
    color: #555;
}
.quote {
    width: 300px;
    font-family: Georgia, "Times New Roman", Times, serif;
    font-style: italic;
    text-indent: -1.8em;
    line-height: 1.5em;
    margin: 1.5em;
}
.quote:before {
    content: "&#x201c;  ";
    font-size: xx-large;
    font-weight: bold;
}
.quote:after {
    content: " &#x201d; ";
    font-size: xx-large;
    font-weight: bold;
}
```

If you now edit your content block again, you'll have a new style ready to be used. Before you select the style, enter some text and select it. As soon as you apply the new style, your text will be wrapped using quotes, making it look like the following screenshot:

Performance perfection when including CSS files

You might have noticed that we've used two different ways to include CSS files. Let's compare them:

- `<?php echo $this->getThemePath() ?>/css/bootstrap.min.css`
- `<?php echo $this->getStylesheet('css/bootstrap.min.css') ?>`

If you look at the output of `getStyleSheet`, you'll see a long address similar to the following:

`/index.php/tools/css/themes/bootstrap1/css/bootstrap.min.css`

You might wonder why there's `index.php` in the address when you include a CSS file. A concrete5 theme can have configurable styles. These styles can be changed in the dashboard without modifying any files. In order to apply the values specified in the concrete5 dashboard, the file has to be processed by some PHP code. This is why we have to use `getStyleSheet`.

However, if you don't intend to use this feature, it will only slow down your site. It's not like a major issue but if it's not necessary, it's recommended to go with `getThemePath`.

Customizable styles

Customizable styles are styles that you can define as a theme developer to allow the user of the theme to change certain values. There are, of course, situations where you want to lock down your design to avoid any bad design choices by the end user. If that's what you're trying to do, ignore customizable styles.

But if you're the kind of person who'd like to give people some freedom, even if they aren't familiar with CSS, this is exactly what you should look at.Let's start with a simple example. Open `main.css` from the currently active theme, probably `bootstrap2`. At the end of the file, append the following code and save all the changes:

```
body {
    /* customize_background */ background-color: #ffffff; /*
customize_background */
}
```

You have to wrap the styles you want to customize with a comment starting with `customize_`. The second part is the name that you'll see in the user interface.

After you've made that change, you can type `themes` in the intelligent search box and click on the first entry. The currently active theme has a slightly different background color; click on its **Customize** button and you'll get to a screen that looks like the following screenshot:

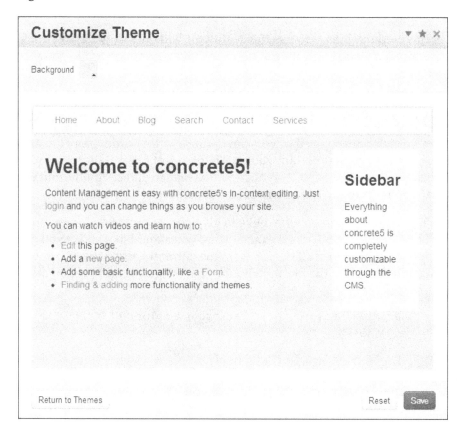

At the top, there's a toolbar where you can see the customizable styles. Click on it and change the value. If you save the new value, you'll see the updated layout.

You can also change the fonts using the customizer; the following example shows you how you have to wrap it:

```
body {
    /* customize_background */ background-color: #ffffff; /*
customize_background */
    /* customize_font */ font: normal normal 13px Arial; /* customize_
font */
}
```

Last but not the least, there's another snippet you can add to your CSS file, which will make it possible to add styles by manually entering them. The complete style for our body tag would then look like the following code:

```
body {
    /* customize_background */ background-color: #ffffff; /*
customize_background */
    /* customize_font */ font: normal normal 13px Arial; /* customize_
font */
    /* customize_miscellaneous */ /* customize_miscellaneous */
}
```

Adding a miscellaneous block will show you a plain textbox where advanced users can manually enter their CSS rules. This is a simple but yet effective way to build a theme that matches the colors of any company. As you've probably experienced before, websites are often cached; if you don't see the new changes immediately, try to clear your cache and try it again.

> **CSS in the root of your theme**
>
> Please note that concrete5 will only parse the customizable styles for CSS files located in the root of the theme. That's also the reason why we've placed the CSS files related to Bootstrap in a subdirectory, but kept our own files in the root of the theme.

Adding more details

We've already created our first theme. It's nothing special; just a rather simple layout based on Bootstrap. In this part, we're going to add more details as we progress step by step.

You don't need all these features in every theme, but it's certainly good to know them to make sure you have some of the available solutions in your mind, in case you need them. As we add new features, we also create new themes. If you want, you can keep on working with `bootstrap2`, but the code in this book is split into different themes.

We just copy the `theme` directory, change the number in `description.txt`, and install the new theme.

Global areas

If you played around with the new theme, you'll probably have noticed that there's an `autonav` block on each page. That basically means that you can have a navigation that differs on each page. This is a great feature, which helps you to create a huge mess.

We could improve that by using page defaults, which allow you to add template-like blocks. Whenever you create a new page, your default navigation would already be included. But that would still make it possible to change the navigation for each page.

As an alternative, concrete5 offers global areas, which have identical content across every page you insert.

Replacing the header area with a global area

Perform the following steps to replace the previously created area to hold our navigation with a global area:

1. Start by making a copy of `bootstrap2` called `bootstrap3`. Now install and activate that theme.

2. Open `elements/header.php` and look for `$areaNav = new Area('Header Nav');`.

3. Replace `new Area` with `new GlobalArea`.

4. Save the changes and go back to your home page.

5. Edit that page to see the new behavior:

If you look closely, you'll see that the link where you can add a new block has changed a bit. Instead of **Add To Header Nav**, it's now called **Add To Sitewide Header Nav**. This is the first indicator that tells you that the changes in this area will be applied to all pages where this area exists. If you click on the navigation block and edit it, you'll see the second hint:

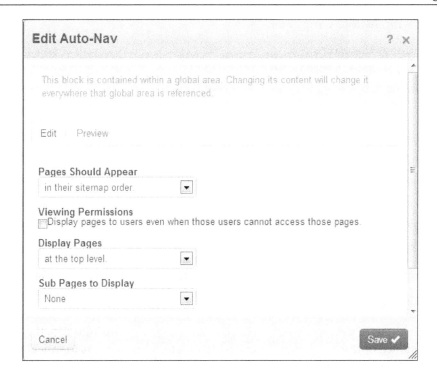

These hints should make it clear that accidental changes in this area will be visible on several pages.

Putting blocks in templates

Working with global areas is great, but if you're a developer you might want to make sure that the navigation remains as you have chosen. This is, of course, also possible. In concrete5 you can create a block by code as well, avoiding the need to add it in the interface.

We'll make that change in a new theme clone called bootstrap4.

Again, we're in elements/header.php; look for the following code:

```
<nav class="navbar">
    <div class="navbar-inner">
        <?php
        $areaNav = new GlobalArea('Header Nav');
        $areaNav->display($c);
        ?>
    </div>
</nav>
```

Replace it with the following code:

```
<nav class="navbar">
    <div class="navbar-inner">
        <?php
        $bt = BlockType::getByHandle('autonav');
        $bt->controller->displayPages = 'top';
        $bt->controller->orderBy = 'display_asc';
        $bt->controller->displaySubPages = 'none';
        $bt->render('view');
        ?>
    </div>
</nav>
```

If you save that change and reload your page, you shouldn't see any change. The previous code should produce the exact same result, but it should also make it impossible for the user to change any settings related to the navigation.

This is how it works:

- `$bt = BlockType::getByHandle('autonav');`: This line gets the instance of the block that you want to create. This name is identical to the directory name of the block. The core block handles can be found in `/concrete/blocks`.

- `$bt->controller->displayPages = 'top';`: Each block has different properties that you have to set. In our example we specify `displayPage`, `orderBy` and `displaySubPages`. We'll look at how you can find those properties in the next section.

- `$bt->render('view');`: Each block can have different templates. The default template is `view` and is always available. You can specify something like `templates/sooperfish` if there's a template called `sooperfish`.

Finding block properties

As mentioned above, if you place a block in the template, you'll have to specify the properties as well. As you can probably imagine, most blocks have different properties and there's not just one collection of properties you can use. Having documentation would be helpful, but with the vast number of blocks we have, it is a pretty big task. Instead, we'll look at how you can figure out the properties on your own.

In our example we're using Google Chrome, but you can use something like Firebug as well, if you're more familiar with it. Let's go through this step by step:

1. Open a page of your choice and switch into the edit mode.

2. Add a new block to any area.

3. Select the auto-nav block.

4. Make all the settings you want in the auto-nav form dialog and use the preview to make sure they work according to your needs.

5. Once you've changed all the fields, click on the first field with your right mouse button and select **Inspect element**:

6. The Google Chrome Developer Tools should pop up with the form element already selected. On the left of the form element is a little arrow to expand its children; click on it and you should get the following information:

```
▼<select name="orderBy">
    <option value="display_asc">in their sitemap order.</option>
    <option value="chrono_desc">with the most recent first.</option>
    <option value="chrono_asc">with the earliest first.</option>
    <option value="alpha_asc">in alphabetical order.</option>
    <option value="alpha_desc">in reverse alphabetical order.</option>
    <option value="display_desc">in reverse sitemap order.</option>
</select>
```

As you can see in the preceding screenshot, the form element has the name `orderBy` this is also the name of the property. If you want to display your pages with the most recent of the updated content first, use `chrono_desc` and you have the value of the property.

If you combine these two, you'll get the following code:

```
$bt->controller->orderBy = 'chrono_desc';
```

Templates for page types

We already have a theme with a navigation, but only one single template. In addition to `default.php`, we need more templates to match the layout for the page type's left sidebar and full width.

As always, we will create a clone of our previous theme `bootstrap4` called `bootstrap5`. We will copy `default.php` into a new file called `left_sidebar.php`. We will basically swap two elements, making the content of `left_sidebar.php` look like the following code:

```php
<?php defined('C5_EXECUTE') or die('Access Denied.') ?>

<?php
$this->inc('elements/header.php');
?>

<div class="row-fluid">
    <div class="span3">
        <div class="well sidebar-nav">
            <?php
            $areaSidebar = new Area('Sidebar');
            $areaSidebar->display($c);
            ?>
        </div>
    </div>
    <div class="span9">
        <?php
        $areaMain = new Area('Main');
        $areaMain->display($c);
        ?>
    </div>
</div>

<?php
$this->inc('elements/footer.php');
?>
```

If you look at the two `div` containers we've swapped, they both have a class starting with `span`. This class is part of the Bootstrap framework and is used to build a basic grid-like layout. Each row should add up to 12 columns, 3 on the left, and 9 on the right.

You can now imagine that if we wanted to build a full width layout, then we'd have to use a class called *span12*. Let's try that by creating another file called `full.php` with this content:

```php
<?php defined('C5_EXECUTE') or die('Access Denied.') ?>

<?php
$this->inc('elements/header.php');
?>

<div class="row-fluid">
    <div class="span12">
        <?php
        $areaMain = new Area('Main');
        $areaMain->display($c);
        ?>
    </div>
</div>

<?php
$this->inc('elements/footer.php');
?>
```

Want to know more about grid layouts?

Grid layouts can be very helpful to create a clean and responsive layout. Splitting content into well split columns can improve the look as well as the usability of your site. The Twitter Bootstrap framework offers a number of different possibilities that make it easy to build such grids. Check out this link for more details:

`http://twitter.github.com/bootstrap/scaffolding.html#fluidGridSystem`

Number of blocks per area

Depending on your layout, it might be enough to have a single block in an area. While this isn't necessary, you can restrict this by specifying the maximum number of blocks per area.

The code needs just one additional line. The old code looks like the following code:

```php
<?php
$areaSidebar = new Area('Sidebar');
$areaSidebar->display($c);
?>
```

It's what we need to tell concrete5 that we'd like to add some content in this spot. The code with a restricted number of blocks looks like the following code:

```php
<?php
$areaSidebar = new Area('Sidebar');
$areaSidebar->setBlockLimit(1);
$areaSidebar->display($c);
?>
```

Once you add this, you'll still see the **Add To Sidebar** link, but if you click on it, you won't be able to add new blocks:

If you want to get rid of the area controls completely, you can disable the design menu. This, of course, only works if you don't need the design menu! If you want to disable the design menu, you have to add an additional line to the configuration file. Open `config/site.php`; it should look like the following code:

```php
<?php
define('DB_SERVER', 'localhost');
define('DB_USERNAME', 'c5book');
```

```php
define('DB_PASSWORD', 'wlx..2AAdapp');
define('DB_DATABASE', 'c5book');
define('PASSWORD_SALT', 'nESkwx4K8g8Lnh5YI4');
```

The actual values on your site are different, but don't worry about them; leave them as they are and insert the highlighted line shown in the following code:

```php
<?php
define('DB_SERVER', 'localhost');
define('DB_USERNAME', 'c5book');
define('DB_PASSWORD', 'wlx..2AAdapp');
define('DB_DATABASE', 'c5book');
define('ENABLE_CUSTOM_DESIGN', false);
define('PASSWORD_SALT', 'nESkwx4K8g8Lnh5YI4');
```

It doesn't matter in which order you define these constants. As long as they are there, it's okay. After you've saved your configuration, you shouldn't see any area controls at all, making it clear that there has to be just one block in the area.

This might not be the most important feature, but imagine if you have a layout with a lot of absolutely positioned containers. Sometimes it happens that the area controls overlap with another container, making the layout messy in the edit mode. If you can restrict the number of blocks, you can avoid that as well. And sometimes it's just nice to make sure your customers can't do too much as well!

Background picture by page attribute

A lot of websites have a big background picture, sometimes even a different picture per page. concrete5 offers a few different possibilities to achieve this; we'll look at one way, which is completely integrated into your theme.

We're going to build this in a way that allows you to specify a picture per page, but use the picture assigned to the home page in case there isn't a page-specific picture.

If you have a large picture in the background, you might want to make sure it scales well and doesn't get stretched to match the size of the browser viewport. This sounds like an easy task, but there's more to it than one might think. Luckily, we don't have to reinvent this wheel and simply use a jQuery plugin for this. This works well with our project as concrete5 internally works with jQuery as well.

One plugin that does a fine job is Supersized. It can be found on the following site:

```
http://www.buildinternet.com/project/supersized/
```

Creating the attribute to hold our picture

First, we need an attribute where we can assign a background picture. Start by entering attributes in the intelligent search box, but make sure you pick the item next to **Pages & Themes**, as shown in the following screenshot:

At the bottom of the screen, select **Image/File** as the type and click on **Add**:

On the next screen, enter all the details needed for the new attribute:

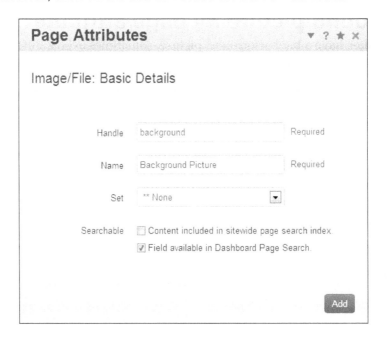

The value you enter in **Handle** is what you'll use to work with the attribute in the code and **Name** is what the end users will see when selecting a background picture.

Assigning attribute to page type

If you earlier worked on a large concrete5 site, you'll probably have had a lot of attributes. At some point, it could get messy if you have to go through the complete list of attributes whenever you want to change a single attribute value.

In concrete5, we can specify the default attributes for every page type, making them visible by default when editing a page of that type. We're going to make sure that the background picture attribute can be selected without having to look through all available attributes.

We start again by using the intelligent search bar; enter page types and select the first entry. Next to every page type is a button called **Settings**. Start with the first page type and you should see a screen like the following screenshot:

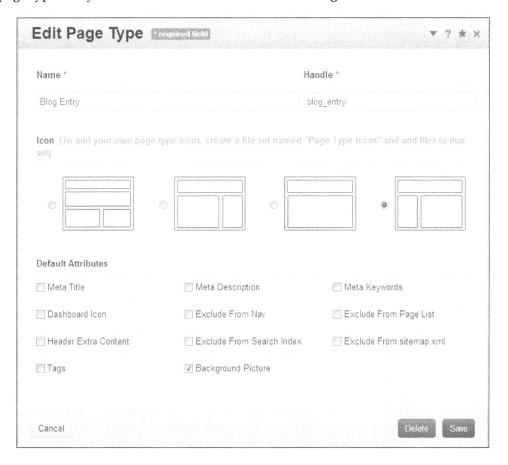

In this screen you can see all available attributes at the bottom. The attributes having the checkbox ticked will be visible by default when you edit the page properties. In our case, we only need the background picture. Tick its checkbox as shown in the previous screenshot and save the change. Do the same for all other page types you've created.

Selecting background pictures

We have our new attribute but there are no values we can work with. Enter sitemap in the intelligent search box and select the first entry **Full Sitemap**. We've defined that if a page has no background picture, we'll use the one assigned to the home page. So let's make sure that this fallback works by clicking on **Home** and then on **Properties**. The following dialog will show up:

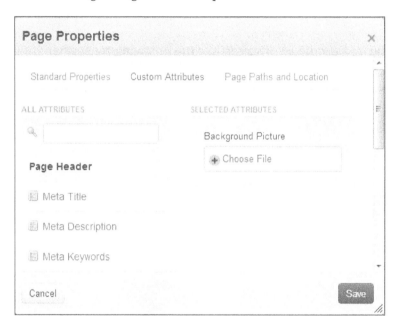

As you can see, our new attribute is on the right and is a part of the already selected attributes. On the left is a list where you can see all available attributes. You can manually assign them to a page by clicking on them. This allows you to easily handle exceptions from the settings you've made in the page types.

Our case is not an exception; we only need to assign a picture to our new attribute. Simply click on **Choose File** and select the picture you want to use as a background for your home page.

Do the same for all pages where you'd like to use a different background picture.

Working with attributes in the theme

Now that we have all the data we need to use a page-specific background picture, let's see how to create the code we need to actually use the data:

1. Create a clone of our previous theme `bootstrap5` called `bootstrap6`. After that, we need the jQuery plugin supersized. You can download the latest version from the following page:

   `http://www.buildinternet.com/project/supersized/download.html`

2. Create two directories in the directory of your theme: `js` and `images`.

3. Extract the minimized JavaScript from `core/js` to the `js` directory in your theme.

4. Copy all images from `core/img` to the `images` directory in your theme.

The plugin needs some additional CSS styles, which we're saving in `main.css` located in the root of your theme. These are the additional lines you have to append:

```
#supersized-loader { position:absolute; top:50%; left:50%; z-index:0;
width:60px; height:60px; margin:-30px 0 0 -30px; text-indent:-999em;
background:url(../images/progress.gif) no-repeat center center;}

#supersized { position:fixed; left:0; top:0; overflow:hidden;
z-index:-999; height:100%; width:100%; }
#supersized img{ width:auto; height:auto; position:relative;
outline:none; border:none; }

#supersized a { z-index:-30; position:fixed; overflow:hidden; top:0;
left:0; width:100%; height:100%; background:#111; display:block; }
#supersized a.image-loading { background:#111 url(../images/progress.
gif) no-repeat center center; width:100%; height:100%; }
```

We already have all the resources we need; we just have to call the JavaScript. This is going to happen in the `header` element. In your theme directory, open `elements/header.php`. We have to insert some code in the header; please note that the following code is not complete. Look for the place where the header element gets closed (`</head>`) in your code:

```
<?php defined('C5_EXECUTE') or die('Access Denied.') ?>

<!DOCTYPE html>
<html lang="en">
    <head>
        <link rel="stylesheet" media="screen" type="text/css"
href="<?php echo $this->getThemePath() ?>/css/bootstrap.min.css" />
```

```
        <link rel="stylesheet" media="screen" type="text/css"
href="<?php echo $this->getStylesheet('main.css') ?>" />

        <!-- Le HTML5 shim, for IE6-8 support of HTML5 elements -->
        <!--[if lt IE 9]>
          <script src="http://html5shim.googlecode.com/svn/trunk/
html5.js"></script        <![endif]-->

        <?php Loader::element('header_required'); ?>

        <?php
        // get background from current page
        $backgroundPicture = $c->getAttribute('background');

        // no picture found, try to get it from the home page
        if (!$backgroundPicture instanceof File) {
            $homePage = Page::getByID(HOME_CID);
            $backgroundPicture = $homePage->getAttribute('backgrou
nd');
        }

        // call supersized if picture found
        if ($backgroundPicture instanceof File) {
            echo '<script src="' . $this->getThemePath() . '/js/
supersized.core.3.2.1.min.js"></script>';
            echo "
            <script>
            $(document).ready(function() {
                $.supersized({slides : [ {image :
'{$backgroundPicture->getURL()}'} ]});

            });
            </script>
            ";
        }
        ?>

    </head>
```

 Check the version of the Supersized plugin as it might have changed by now. In the code above, it's 3.2.1; make sure it matches with the name of the file you've extracted before.

After you've made all these changes, you can reload your site and will see a nicely adjusted background picture. If you want, you can go ahead and implement more features from Supersized. The plugin allows you to build a slideshow, which runs in the background of your site and does much more; check out the following documentation to get a list of all the available options:

```
http://www.buildinternet.com/project/supersized/docs.html
```

Page-specific variables

There are a number of different values you might want to fetch from the current page object. As you've seen above, we can get the value of an attribute to display a page-specific background picture. That's of course not the end; there are a lot more possibilities.

We're going to look at some of them, mostly those you can use in your theme to add some nice gimmicks to your site.

Getting page name and description

Sometimes it can be helpful if you don't have to enter the title of the page in the content again. The page already has a name and if this name works for the title in the content as well, we can use that value and make sure that every page has a title formatted in the same way.

If you want to test the code yourself, open `full.php` in `bootstrap6` and make it look like the following:

```php
<?php defined('C5_EXECUTE') or die('Access Denied.') ?>

<?php
$this->inc('elements/header.php');
?>

<div class="row-fluid">
    <div class="span12">
        <?php
        echo '<h1>' . $c->getCollectionName() . '</h1>';

        $areaMain = new Area('Main');
        $areaMain->display($c);
        ?>
    </div>
```

```
</div>

<?php
$this->inc('elements/footer.php');
?>
```

We only added one line of code. Let's quickly look at the elements we've used. $c is a global variable you can use if you're in the context of a page. It simply refers to the current page. From that object, we've used a method called getCollectionName() to get the value entered in the title property of the page.

In case you also want to print the description property, copy the line we've added and replace getCollectionName() with getCollectionDescription().

Checking the edit mode

By now, you'll probably have seen the toolbar on top of your site a few times, while you were logged in. This toolbar is what makes it easy to change something on your current page, without having to navigate through a technical backend.

However, this toolbar can also cause some troubles. It might happen that you can't click on every element of your page if there's an overlapping toolbar on top of it. You can avoid that by checking if the current page is in the edit mode and add a dummy element to push down the content of your page.

The following code checks if the current page is in the edit mode and if it is, prints an element with a height of 49 pixels:

```
<?php if ($c->isEditMode()) { ?>
<div style="min-height: 49px"></div>
<?php } ?>
```

Getting the current page type

Sometimes you have to use CSS styles that differ per page type. What if the full width page type should have a different background color? We could use an attribute like we did before, but we can also hardcode this in the CSS file.

We're going to create a CSS class that is generated with the handle of the collection type. Let's have a look at an example before we look at the code. Assuming we have a page type called Full with the handle named full. We'd want to use this, to have a body tag that looks like the following:

```
<body class="page_type_full">
```

Using this class we can use the CSS rules, as shown in the following code:

```
.page_type_full { background: #ccc; }
```

Open `header.php` in the `elements` directory of your theme and look for `<body>` and replace it with the following code:

```
<body class="page_type_<?php echo $c->getCollectionTypeHandle()?>">
```

Reload the page and you'll have a CSS class starting with `page_type_` and ending with the handle of the selected page type.

Summary

In this chapter we've covered a lot of different things related to the creation of themes. You've seen a few ideas about things you can do in concrete5 that might help you to come up with some new ideas of your own as well. You don't have to remember every detail as we continue, but understanding the basic principles of working with areas and elements is essential.

This book is about themes, but the journey isn't finished yet. While we've already covered the most important part, we still have to look at how we can customize some other elements in concrete5.

Most themes you download or buy in the marketplace not only contain what we've seen in this chapter, but also contain some styles to customize the look and feel of the blocks as well as certain pages of the concrete5 core.

4
Styling Single Pages

So far, we've already covered what you need to build a basic site in the look you desire. In concrete5, you'll find more elements like blocks and something called single pages. You can build all of that on your own, but sometimes you just want to make sure that the existing single pages match the look of the theme. An example would be the page shown if the requested page couldn't be found — the so called "404 error" page.

In this chapter, we're going to look at these pages and make sure they match the look of your theme. We'll cover the following topics:

- A few words about single pages in general to get a better understanding about them
- The process to create a new single page
- The steps that are necessary to install a single page
- How to change the look of a single page
- Overriding the parts of a single page from the core

What is a single page?

A single page shares a lot with the pages we've created before; but there are reasons as to why you should consider using or creating a single page instead of a page you create in the sitemap:

- Just like the name says, a single page is located in only one place. It will only have one address (for example, /login) and therefore only appear once in your whole site.
- If you have some custom code that is needed in one particular spot, use a single page to avoid any kind of redundancy.

The code of a single page is usually not part of your theme; they are either part of the site, a package, or the core. This makes sense because you don't want to lose the ability to log in to your site just because you remove a theme.

The best example of a single page is probably the dashboard. There are tons of screens where you can create users, change settings, and much more. Would it make sense to have the same screen to create a user in different places? Hardly; and that's why they are all single pages.

Creating our own single page

When you create concrete5 themes, you'll probably not have to create your own single pages on a daily basis; but just keep in mind the reasons why you should use them and how they work on a basic level, so you can easily change their layout. This is why we're going to create a very basic single page on our own.

Our single page will only show a simple form and display a message once you submit the form. First we have to create a new file; but this time, it will be in the root of your site and not within the themes!

In the single_pages directory, create a new file called test_form.php with the following content:

```php
<?php
defined('C5_EXECUTE') or die('Access Denied.');

$fh = Loader::helper('form');

if ($this->controller->getTask() == 'send') {
    if (isset($message)) {
        $th = Loader::helper('text');
        echo '<div class="alert">';
        echo $th->sanitize($message);
        echo '</div>';
    }
} else {
    $action = $this->action('send');
    echo '<form method="post" action="' . $action . '">';

    echo $fh->label('name', t('Name'));
    echo $fh->text('name');

    echo $fh->submit('submit', t('Submit'));

    echo '</form>';
}
```

Creating a file in `single_pages` is already enough for a single page to work, but in our case, we want to add some logic as well. In theory, you could do all that in the file you just created, but we want to keep our code nice and tidy, and follow the MVC pattern whenever possible. This means that we want to use a controller to handle the data processing.

To do this, add a new file with the same name `test_form.php` but this time, in the root directory, `controllers`. Put this content in it and save the file:

```php
<?php
defined('C5_EXECUTE') or die('Access Denied.');

class TestFormController extends Controller {
    public function send() {
        $this->set('message', t('Thanks %s!', $this->post('name')));
    }
}
```

This is what happens in these two files:

- `Loader::helper('form')`: In concrete5 you can find lots of helpers to simplify common tasks. The `form` helper is just one of them. We're using it to print our form elements, in this case: a label, a textbox, and a submit button. More information about the available helpers can be found at `http://www.concrete5.org/documentation/developers/helpers/core-user-interface/`.

- `$this->controller->getTask()`: Our form can be submitted and has to react on this action. As a reaction to it, we also want to display a different content. Using the `getTask` method, we can check the current action of the controller and handle the output in the single page accordingly.

- `$th->sanitize($message)`: As the name suggests, this method sanitizes the input of the form. Never trust the data you get from a browser. Insufficient input validation can result in various kinds of code injection, leading to stolen user credentials and other security issues. You might have heard of **Cross-Site-Scripting (XSS)** before. This is why you should use `$th->sanitize`.

- `$this->action('send')`: In order to make sure our form data gets forwarded to our `send` controller method, we simply use this method. Make sure that there's a method in the controller matching the name of the first parameter. The `getTask()` method, which we've explained earlier, connects to this.

- `$this->set('message'...`: This method forwards the content of a variable to the single page. Whatever name you use in the first parameter will be available as a variable in the single page; $message, in this case.

- `t('Thanks %s!', $this->post('name'))`: The t-function is probably one of the most commonly used functions in concrete5 you can find. This function ensures that every string can be translated. With the help of a scanning process, all these strings are collected and are available for translation. The t-function uses a parameter system identical to the one used in sprint to replace placeholders. For more examples, check http://php. net/manual/en/function.sprintf.php.

>
> **Want to help translate concrete5?**
>
> There are a number of translations available for concrete5, but there are still a few languages left if you want help with the translations. Check this page for more information:
>
> http://www.concrete5.org/developers/translate/

As you can see in the preceding code example, we've created a variable called message in our controller to be used in the output of the single page. Being able to forward any kind of data in any kind of variable name gives you some flexibility, but also has the disadvantage that you never know what kind of variables you have to process in the single page. This can be a bit annoying if you just want to override the style in an existing single page. This means that you sometimes have to look through the controller code to determine the variables you have to work with. These controllers are usually in one of the following directories:

- `/concrete/core/controllers/single_pages/`
- `/packages/<package-name>/controllers/`
- `/controllers/`
- `/updates/<concrete5-version>/core/controllers/single_pages/`

There's a bit of digging involved, but at the benefit of having a lot of freedom when creating single pages.

Working with subdirectories

If you look at the code you've created, you'll see a file called `test_form.php` in both the directories, `controllers` and `single_pages`. If you need to create a more complex structure of single pages, you can also create subdirectories. Instead of having a file in `/controllers/test_form.php`, you can also have a file such as `/controllers/test_form/controller.php` which will be accessible from the same address. The single page can also be moved from `/single_pages/test_form.php` to `/single_pages/test_form/view.php`. Note that `view.php` and `controller.php` are the default file, names you can use to access the first level, but you can also add more files such as `/controllers/test_form/detail.php` and `/single_pages/test_form/detail.php`.

If you want to know more about this, check this detaillled tutorial about single pages: `http://www.concrete5.org/documentation/how-tos/developers/build-a-single-page-powered-editing-interface-for-concrete5/`

Installing single pages

A single page, which is a part of the package, has to be installed using code; but a single page in the root of your site, like the one we just created, can be installed on the dashboard. To do this, enter `single pages` in the intelligent search box and select the first entry.

In the screen you can see now, you have to register your single page. This is necessary because concrete5 is a database-based CMS and needs to know where to find its pages. Our single page is located in `/single_pages/test_form.php`. When installing a single page, you don't have to repeat the first folder and remove the file extension.

In our case, we simply enter `test_form` as shown in the following screenshot:

After you add the new single page, you still can't click on the link which you'll see right underneath the form. If you do, you'll get an error. In order to display a styled single page, your theme needs another file called `view.php`, which is necessary as soon as there's a single page to be displayed in the look of your theme. Such a single page can be a part of your site but also a part of a package. Just have a look at the next section.

This single page is, of course, not really useful but you should at least understand how a basic single page works, and how to use your existing PHP knowledge to move your code into the concrete5 framework.

Changing the single page layout

Every single page has its own HTML code, which we're not going to change in the beginning. In a lot of situations, it's enough if you can add your own header, footer, and CSS code to change the layout of a single page. But don't worry, we're going to look at a slick way that allows you to change the HTML code as well.

Adding view.php to your theme

In order to style single pages, we have to create a file called `view.php`. Before we create this file, here's an illustration which shows you the process that a single page uses to show some output:

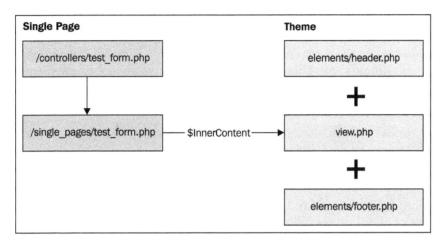

In the left column is the single page, the controller that prepares all the data, and the actual single page file that creates the content element specific for this page and stores it in a variable called `$innerContent`. This output is then wrapped using the common elements we already used in our theme. The single page output isn't a complete HTML document; it's just a small part and therefore fits well into our existing theme as all other page templates work in the same way. As soon as we wrap it using the theme elements, it becomes a complete document.

Let's create that missing piece by making another clone of our theme *bootstrap6* called *bootstrap7*. Don't forget to install and activate this theme.

Within the new theme, create a new file called `view.php` with the following content:

```php
<?php defined('C5_EXECUTE') or die('Access Denied.') ?>

<?php
$this->inc('elements/header.php');
?>

<div class="row-fluid">
    <div class="span12">
        <?php
        echo $innerContent;
        ?>
    </div>
```

```
</div>

<?php
$this->inc('elements/footer.php');
?>
```

As you can see, this file is almost identical to `full.php`; we only replaced the area with `echo $innerContent`. If you compare the new file with the illustration above, you should see how the different elements get together. You can keep using areas, even if it's in a single page. This can be very helpful if you want to generate the output using program code, but also keep a part editable through the concrete5 editing system.

Now that we have our final piece in the theme, you can open the new single page using an address like the following:

```
http://www.your-site.com/test_form/
```

Enter something in the form and you'll see the output again after you submit the form.

> **Almost mandatory view.php**
>
> While it's technically not necessary to have a file called `view.php` in your theme, it's pretty much a must for most themes. It's not only required when you create your own single page, but also if you install a package that installs single pages. As it can be difficult to know if a package will install a single page, it's recommended to create `view.php` for every theme.

Applying the theme to single pages

Now that you understand how a single page works, let's have a look at how we can change the layout of a single page included in the concrete5 core. We start by telling concrete5 for which pages we want to use our own theme.

To do this, create a new file called `site_theme_paths.php` in the `config` directory in the root of your site, if it's not already there. There's already another file called `site.php` in it. Once you've created the file, put this content in it:

```php
<?php
$v = View::getInstance();

$v->setThemeByPath('/page_not_found', 'bootstrap7');
$v->setThemeByPath('/login', 'bootstrap7');
```

If you now open a page that doesn't exist, you'll see a "page not found" information styled using your theme. There's nothing else to be done to change the look of the 404 page.

Let's have a look at the login page where you have to do a bit more work. If you now open http://www.your-site.com/login, you can see the new layout of the login page. Try to log in using a non-existent username and password. Previously, you saw a message telling you that your username or password is invalid, but with the new layout, there's no such information.

As we've seen in the first part of this chapter, a controller of a single page can use any variable it wants. If you want, you can practice concrete5 code reading but for those who want the shortcut, look at the highlighted line in the following code snippet. It's what you'll need to make the error messages on the login screen appear:

```php
<?php defined('C5_EXECUTE') or die('Access Denied.') ?>

<?php
$this->inc('elements/header.php');
?>

<div class="row-fluid">
    <div class="span12 well">
        <?php
        Loader::element('system_errors', array('error' => $error));

        echo $innerContent;
        ?>
    </div>
</div>

<?php
$this->inc('elements/footer.php');
?>
```

That's all you need for a custom layout in the 404 and login page. If you want to style another page, just go to the single page section in the dashboard, look for the path of the page, and copy paste it into site_theme_paths.php as a new line, and you have your new layout.

Overriding the single page's HTML output

If you don't like the look of the login page, you can always add some lines to your CSS file to change it, but there's another way. We're going to override the whole single page template this time. It's not always clear as to why you should keep using CSS or override the template. It's just important to keep in mind that with this approach, we're going to copy quite a few lines of code. If something changes in a future version of concrete5, you might have to check your custom single page template as well.

Before we change anything, let's have a look at the following illustration. It shows the flow that the login single page goes through by default:

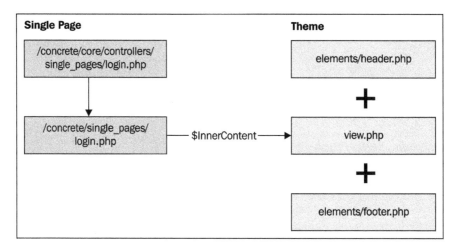

It's pretty much the same as shown in the first illustration a few pages earlier. Now, let's override it; but first, create another clone of your theme *bootstrap7* called *bootstrap8*. Make sure you change the theme name in /config/ site_theme_paths. php as well.

In the new theme, create a new file called login.php in the same level where view. php is located.

```php
<?php defined('C5_EXECUTE') or die('Access Denied.') ?>

<?php
$this->inc('elements/header.php');
?>

<div class="row-fluid">
    <div class="span12 well">
        <?php
```

```
Loader::element('system_errors', array('error' => $error));

/*<<<Content of /concrete/single_pages/login.php>>>*/
?>
</div>
</div>

<?php
$this->inc('elements/footer.php');
?>
```

Note that the code above isn't complete. Make sure you replace the highlighted line with the content of the file `/concrete/single_pages/login.php`. Once you've done that, you can see that you've created a lot of redundant code. This might cause some update issues in the future, but allows you to change the last bit of the login page. The login page is probably not going to change completely, overriding it shouldn't be too risky. However, it's always a good thing to check the files you've overridden before you upgrade to a newer version of concrete5. Make all the changes you want and reload the login page and you'll see that you just figured out an easy way to customize another part of concrete5 without a lot of effort.

Now that you've created another file in your theme, the flow that the login page goes through is a bit different. Check the following illustration and try to compare it to the previous illustration:

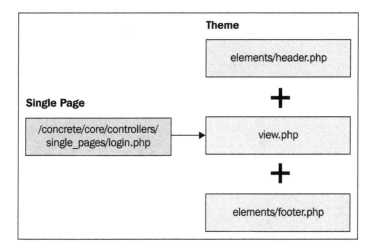

Summary

If you got to this point and have carefully read and studied the idea behind the single pages, you should be able to customize the look and feel of this concrete5 element. Customizing single pages is something that a lot of theme developers tend to forget, but it's easy to do as you can use an almost identical recipe for all your sites. Mostly, you just have to create the `view.php` in your theme and specify the pages to be changed in `site_theme_paths.php`.

Play around with the single pages features offered by concrete5, find a way that suits you and you'll be able to use it on several sites without a lot of work. If you try to keep the structure of your themes the same, you get the single page styling pretty much for free.

If you want to remember what a single page is, keep in mind that the whole dashboard has been built using single pages. Why? It's mainly because the functionality on each page is unique and contains some rather specific code not used in other places.

You might wonder why you're still not at the end of this book about concrete5 themes. Creating a concrete5 theme including some layout customization should be in your skill set by now, but there's more. When you previously managed the content of your site, you've added, changed, and removed blocks. Each block can have several layouts, allowing you to customize even more. Check out the next chapter and you'll learn how to change the block output in no time.

5
Styling the Block Output

The blocks you can freely place in the content areas of concrete5 are very powerful and have almost no limit regarding their flexibility. This also means that they can display a lot of different things, starting from a simple text output to a video, a complex form, picture galleries, and even data from other systems.

This flexibility also means that certain blocks can have a lot of output including some formatting, which might not fit into your theme's layout. In such a case you can either try to change it by using a CSS file, and if this doesn't work, add or override a new block template. The latter is exactly what we're going to look at in this chapter.

We'll cover the following topics in this chapter:

- Overriding block templates to change the output of an existing block
- How to use CSS and JavaScript files in a block template
- How to put a block template in a package
- An example showing you how to change the `autonav` block into a drop-down navigation
- A template for the page list block which adds a category filter

Overriding block templates

Before we start creating our own block templates, we want to look at the files we'll either find or create. Knowing where to look for the right template is a good start, especially for experienced PHP programmers, as most of the templates are rather easy to read and don't need a lot of explanation once you've found them.

Let's start by looking at the following directory structure:

The first directory /blocks is located in the root of your site and might contain custom blocks you've created yourself or installed manually. One level below, in the concrete directory, you can see some blocks available in the concrete5 core. As mentioned before, never change a file underneath the /concrete directory, as this is part of the core.

When working with a block template, it's important to understand that you can override the core elements in concrete5. What does this mean?

Let's start with a simple example:

Copy the view.php file from /concrete/blocks/content to /blocks/content. You probably have to create the directory content first. The structure should look like the following screenshot:

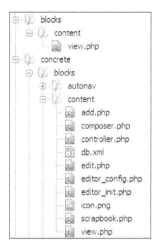

By copying this file from the core we're overriding the default view of the content block. When rendering the output of a block, concrete5 looks for the `view.php` file in the root directory `/blocks` and only processes the one located in the `/concrete` directory if this can't be found.

Disabling the override cache

As you can imagine, looking for files in a lot of different places can take a bit of time, especially if you have a lot of blocks and packages installed. In order to improve this, concrete5 has an override cache. Before you start developing and testing new templates, make sure you disable it, otherwise you'll run into a lot of small problems relating to the file not being found. Type `cache settings` in the intelligent search box and and select the first entry. In this screen, tick the radio button **off** next to **override cache** and save the changes.

You can already make changes to the file you just created and once you reload your page, you'll see the changes immediately. This is the default process you need to follow if you want to override the default core block template.

Additional block templates

If you don't want to override the default template but rather add a new one, you'll have to do almost the same thing and just rename the file. If you'd want to have another template for the content block, in addition to the default template which we overrode, copy the `view.php` file from `/concrete/blocks/content` to `/blocks/content/templates` and rename it as `new_template.php`. Please note that you have to put custom templates in a new directory called `templates`, unlike the default template `view.php` which is one level higher.

After you've copied the template, go to a page of your choice and edit it. If there's no content block in the page, add one first. Once you have a content block in your page, click on it, and you'll see a menu like the following screenshot:

After you have clicked on the **Custom Template** option, you'll see a dialog like the following screenshot:

As you can see, the filename `new_template.php` is converted to **New Template**. Underscores are removed and followed by a capital letter, and the file extension is hidden as well. This is done for all the templates and allows you to make sure the actual name shown in the dialog looks a bit less technical.

Block templates with CSS and JavaScript

If you just copy the `view.php` file, you'll be able to change the markup; but if you want to add some template-specific CSS, you shouldn't just put them in the `view.php` file. As soon as you place a block in one page twice, you'd have the same CSS code in the page twice, as the content of the `view.php` file is printed for each block. That is why you should create a separate file for this.

A template can contain JavaScript as well as CSS files, which are automatically included with the selected template. The following screenshot contains a demo template with all the elements that are automatically included by concrete5:

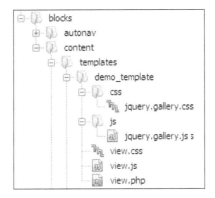

The three files `view.php`, `view.js`, and `view.css` must have the filename view. All files in the `css` directory ending with `.css` and all files in the `js` directory ending with `.js` are automatically included as well. These JavaScript and CSS files are included only once in the head of the rendered page, even if you add multiple instances of the block with this template.

Content block in a box

We already know what's most important when creating a new block template. Now we're going to use this knowledge to create a new template for the content block, which will only show a small link by default and reveal the actual content in a box.

To do this, we're going to use an existing jQuery plugin called **fancyBox**. It's free to use on private and non-commercial sites, and offers a wide variety of options allowing you to include a simple gallery, formatted content, and even dynamic elements — like videos — in a nicely styled box.

First, you have to download the fancyBox plugin from `http://fancyapps.com/fancybox`. Next, you have to create a new directory called `fancybox` in/blocks/content/templates and extract some files from the source directory of fancyBox into the `css` and `js` directories as shown in the following screenshot:

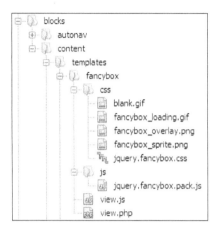

Everything else in the `fancybox` directory isn't required for our purpose. There are two files though, which you have to create. Firstly, the `view.js` file should be created as follows:

```
$(document).ready(function() {
    $(".fancybox-content-link").fancybox();
});
```

As you can see, this file is very simple. It's only purpose is to initialize the fancyBox plugin. There are a lot of options you can use to customize the behavior of the fancyBox. The following code is an alternative that you can use for the `view.js` file that shows you additional properties you can use:

```
$(document).ready(function() {
    $(".fancybox-content-link").fancybox({
        maxWidth : 400,
        maxHeight : 200,
        fitToView : false,
        autoSize : false,
        closeClick : false,
        openEffect : 'elastic',
        closeEffect : 'elastic'
    });
});
```

For a complete list of options, please visit `http://fancyapps.com/fancybox/`.

The last file we're going to need is the `view.php` file with the following content:

```php
<?php defined('C5_EXECUTE') or die("Access Denied.");
$content = $controller->getContent();
echo "<a
  href=\"#fancybox-content-{$bID}\"
  class=\"fancybox-content-link\">Show more</a>";
echo "<div
  id=\"fancybox-content-{$bID}\"
  class=\"fancybox-content\"
  style=\"display: none;\">";
echo $content;
echo "</div>";
?>
```

This code wraps the existing content block output in the `$content` variable in new `div` with an ID like `fancybox-content-123`. Why is the number `123` there? In concrete5, each block instance has a unique number. This number is available in a variable called `$bID` from within the block template. We use this because we want to make sure that a click on **Show more** displays just the content belonging to the actual link, and not the content from other links. You don't have to make your code unique by using the `$bID` variable, as long as you only have one instance per block on your page. However, since concrete5 offers this flexibility, you should try to make sure that you can place every block and also every block template on one page several times. After all, you can never really know what your customers are going to do.

The output of the previous code is going to look like the following code snippet:

```html
<a href="#fancybox-content-123">Show more</a>
<div id="fancybox-content-123" style="display:none;">
  Content
</div>
```

As you can see in this example, the anchor in the link points to the ID of the element containing the actual text. In combination with little JavaScript, this is everything the fancyBox plugin needs to know to display a dialog box like the following screenshot:

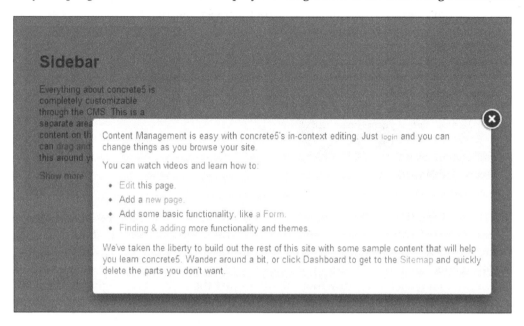

Overriding blocks in packages

The block templates we've created were always in the top-level directory /blocks. This works fine for your personal site, but if you want to distribute your theme or block templates, you might want to wrap these templates in a package. Just like themes, blocks, and jobs, you can also put a simple block template in a package. This is mandatory if you want to publish it in the concrete5 marketplace; and it could also help you to manage your own add-ons, as you know that they have to be installed in the /packages directory.

If you've already built a package, you simply have to move your templates into that directory and as soon as you install the package, they are available to be used.

For example: If you have a template called new_template.php in /blocks/content/templates/, move that file to /packages/your-package/blocks/content/templates and your template is nicely packed, ready for the marketplace.

You can get more information about packages from http://www.concrete5.org/documentation/developers/system/packages.

Changing the navigation

In concrete5, you can easily create a navigation using the `autonav` block, which will display a specified set of pages from the sitemap in a list or tree-like structure.

This block displays a very basic structure without too much styling. It's a great start as it doesn't contain a lot of distracting codes but it also means that you'll probably want to add a bit more of your own style, and therefore making sure it goes well with the layout of your theme.

The default template generates a structure using the `<ul>` and `<li>` elements similar to the following code snippet:

```
<ul class="nav">
  <li>Home</li>
  <li>Services
    <ul>
      <li>Mobile App Services</li>
    </ul>
  </li>
</ul>
```

If you can, use some CSS to change the look according to your needs. It's very likely, though, that you'll encounter a situation where you need different classes depending on the state. It might even be possible that you want to change the actual output if you want to display a picture, instead of just text in the navigation. The more you work with concrete5, the more situations you'll find where you want to change the `autonav` block.

In our case, we're going to look at an example where we have to change the output to work with JavaScript. The framework **bootstrap** — which we've used to style our site — offers not just some basic CSS elements, but also some JavaScript components. We're going to use a component called `dropdown`. Check this page for an example: `http://twitter.github.com/bootstrap/javascript.html#dropdowns`.

Before we start creating our new block template, let's have a look at a basic bootstrap dropdown:

```
<div class="dropdown">
  <a class="dropdown-toggle"
    role="button"
    data-toggle="dropdown"
    href="#">
    More
  <b class="caret"></b>
```

```
        </a>
        <ul class="dropdown-menu" role="menu">
           <li><a href="http://www.google.com/">Help</a></li>
        </ul>
     </div>
```

On a page where bootstrap is included, this code will produce the following result:

As you can see, we have to add few attributes to let bootstrap know what each element is supposed to do. The `data-toggle="dropdown"` attribute on a link or button is needed to toggle the dropdown. The submenu then has two more attributes, `role` and `class`, to make it a submenu. That's all we need for a basic dropdown.

In order to be able to integrate this navigation in concrete5, we have to make a few changes in the HTML code generated by *autonav*. We're starting by creating a new `autonav` block template. Copy the `view.php` file from `/concrete/blocks/autonav` to `/blocks/autonav/templates` and rename it as `bootstrap.php`. If you open this file, you'll see a lot of comments which explain the default block template very well. You might want to read these comments to get a better understanding of the default template before you continue. In short, the template receives an array of pages in a variable called `$navItems`. By looping through every element in this variable, we can build the HTML structure we need.

The complete code of the `bootstrap.php` file without all the comments looks similar to the following code:

```php
<?php
defined('C5_EXECUTE') or die('Access Denied.');
$navItems = $controller->getNavItems();

/*** STEP 1 of 2: Determine all CSS classes (only 2 are enabled by
default, but you can un-comment other ones or add your own) ***/
foreach ($navItems as $ni) {
  $classesLi = array();
  $classesUl = array();
  $classesA = array();
  $attributesA = array()
    if ($ni->isCurrent || $ni->inPath) {
       // class for the page currently being viewed
```

```php
            $classesLi[] = 'active';
        }

        if ($ni->hasSubmenu) {
            // class for items that have dropdown submenus
            $classesLi[]   = 'dropdown';
            $classesA[]    = 'dropdown-toggle ';
            $attributesA[] = 'data-toggle="dropdown"';
            $classesUl[]   = 'dropdown-menu';
            $ni->url       = '#';
        }

        // Put all classes together into one space-separated string
        $ni->classesLi   = implode(" ", $classesLi);
        $ni->classesA    = implode(" ", $classesA);
        $ni->classesUl   = implode(" ", $classesUl);
        $ni->attributesA = implode(" ", $attributesA);
    }


    //*** Step 2 of 2: Output menu HTML ***/
    echo "<ul class=\"nav\">";

    foreach ($navItems as $ni) {

        echo "<li class=\"{$ni->classesLi}\">";
        echo "<a href=\"{$ni->url}\"
                target=\"{$ni->target}\"
                class=\"{$ni->classesA}\" {$ni->attributesA}>
            {$ni->name}</a>";

        if ($ni->hasSubmenu) {
            echo "<ul class=\"{$ni->classesUl}\">";
        } else {
            echo "</li>";
            echo str_repeat("</ul></li>", $ni->subDepth);
        }
    }

    echo "</ul>";
```

This code isn't much different from the original template, but let's have a closer look at the following two highlighted details:

- `$ni->isCurrent || $ni->inPath`: We use two properties to check if the current element in the loop should be marked as `active` or not. The first property `$ni->isCurrent` will be true if the element in the loop is the currently viewed page. The `$ni->inPath` property is true if the current element in the loop is a part of the path of the current page. If you're currently on `/about/help`, the page object for `/about` would be in the path; hence the `$ni->inPath` property would be true.

- `$ni->hasSubmenu`: This property is true if the current element in the loop has subelements. This is necessary because we have to add some attributes to our element as soon as there's a submenu. We're filling a number of arrays with properties and printing them in the element in the loop a few lines later.

Working with the drop-down block template

Our template needs two more changes in our theme. There's JavaScript from bootstrap, which we should include, and there's also a modification in the `autonav` call we currently have in our `header.php` file.

As you've seen before, we can include JavaScript in a block template—you probably will wonder why we're not doing this in this case. There's a simple explanation for this. The bootstrap JavaScript contains a lot of components, not just the drop-down menu we're using in this example. If you build another block template where you need another bootstrap component, and include JavaScript in the block template, you'll end up having the same JavaScript twice in your page. Because of this, we're putting JavaScript in the theme to make sure we don't have any redundancy in the future. The downside of this is that the block template will only work with a theme that includes the bootstrap JavaScript. That's not an issue, just something you have to be aware of if you want to use the template on another site.

As always, let's create a new clone of our theme *bootstrap8* called *bootstrap9*. Also, make sure you don't forget to install and activate it.

There's just one file we have to modify. Open the `header.php` file from `/elements` and make sure it looks like the following code, the changes are highlighted:

```php
<?php defined('C5_EXECUTE') or die('Access Denied.') ?>

<!DOCTYPE html>
<html lang="en">
  <head>
```

```
    <link rel="stylesheet" media="screen" type="text/css"
href="<?php echo $this->getThemePath() ?>/css/bootstrap.min.css"
/>
    <link rel="stylesheet" media="screen" type="text/css"
href="<?php echo $this->getStylesheet('main.css') ?>" />
    <link rel="stylesheet" media="screen" type="text/css"
href="<?php echo $this->getThemePath() ?>/typography.css" />

    <!-- Le HTML5 shim, for IE6-8 support of HTML5 elements -->
    <!--[if lt IE 9]>
      <script
src="http://html5shim.googlecode.com/svn/trunk/html5.js"></script>
    <![endif]-->

    <?php Loader::element('header_required'); ?>

    <?php
    // get background from current page
    $backgroundPicture = $c->getAttribute('background');

    // no picture found, try to get it from the home page
    if (!$backgroundPicture instanceof File) {
      $homePage = Page::getByID(HOME_CID);
      $backgroundPicture = $homePage->getAttribute('background');
    }

    // call supersized if picture found
    if ($backgroundPicture instanceof File) {
      echo '<script src="' . $this->getThemePath() .
'/js/supersized.core.3.2.1.min.js"></script>';
      echo "
        <script>
        $(document).ready(function() {
          $.supersized({slides : [ {image : '{$backgroundPicture-
>getURL()}'} ]});

        });
        </script>
        ";
    }

    // add bootstrap JavaScript for our drop-down navigation
    echo '<script src="' . $this->getThemePath() .
'/js/bootstrap.min.js"></script>';
```

```
    ?>

  </head>

  <body>

    <div id="wrapper">
      <nav class="navbar">
        <div class="navbar-inner">
          <?php
          $bt = BlockType::getByHandle('autonav');
          $bt->controller->displayPages = 'top';
          $bt->controller->orderBy = 'display_asc';
          $bt->controller->displaySubPages = 'all';
          $bt->controller->displaySubPageLevels = 'custom';
          $bt->controller->displaySubPageLevelsNum = 2;
          $bt->render('templates/bootstrap');
          ?>
        </div>
      </nav>
    </div>

    <div class="container-fluid">
```

The first change is the JavaScript that was mentioned previously. The second change is a bit trickier. Let's have a look at all the changes we've made to that block:

- `displaySubPages = 'all'`: In a drop-down navigation, we have to print items, even if they aren't visible. This means that we have to display all subpages, not just those that are beneath the current page.

- `displaySubPageLevels = 'custom'`: If you have a site with tons of pages, it can take a while to build a complete structure with all the pages. By setting a fixed number to the page levels, we can make sure that the `autonav` block doesn't have to fetch every page object. This makes sure that your site won't slow down if you add more pages.

- `$bt->render('templates/bootstrap')`: Previously, we've used `view` instead of `templates/bootstrap`. `View` refers to the default template file `view.php` in the block directory; but we want to use our new template `templates/bootstrap.php`, and therefore have to change that value.

Once you've saved all these changes and activated the new theme, you'll see a navigation like the following screenshot:

Global areas

If you don't feel very comfortable with code, you skip the last part of the code which starts with `BlockType::getByHandle('aut onav')` and use a global area. As we've seen before, a global area contains blocks which are shown in every page containing the global area. This is another way to place a navigation on every page of a site. Simply use the following code and add the `autonav` block using the concrete5 insite editing system:

```
$areaNav = new GlobalArea('Header Nav');
$areaNav->display($c);
```

Creating a portfolio list with filter

As you might have guessed, the page list block allows you to build a list of pages. This list is flat and can't display any kind of hierarchy like the `autonav` block does. However, you can add a few filter options in the page list block to show only a certain type of page. If you look at the following screenshot, you can see a setting that will display 10 pages of the `Blog Entry` type:

Such a list could be used to display the latest news, articles, a list of team members, products, and probably a lot more if you consult your imagination. When you add this block, it will show you a simple list of pages with the page description you entered when you created the page, and of course, a link to bring you to the detail page. This is okay but might be a bit too simple. What if the list gets long and confusing? Wouldn't it be nice if there was a filter that your visitor could use in order to hide those pages he doesn't need?

As you might have already guessed, that's no problem with concrete5. In our example, we're going to use a JavaScript called **quicksand**. You can find a few examples as well as some documentation on `http://razorjack.net/quicksand/`.

Adding portfolio attributes

We want to categorize each page and therefore need an attribute on each page being shown in the list. To do this, type `attributes` in the intelligent search box and click on the entry next to `Pages & Themes`. At the bottom of the screen, add a new attribute using the `Select` type. Enter the values shown in the following screenshot to create the attribute:

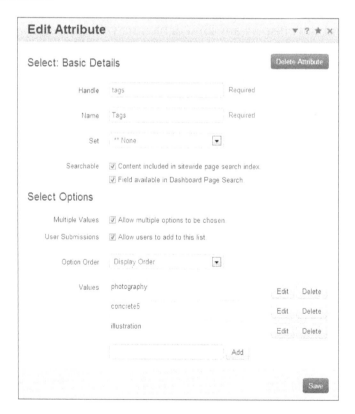

Here, `Handle` is what you'll need in the code to access the attributes, `Name` is what the user sees, and at the bottom you have some options that you can change to suit your needs. You can predefine the values and/or allow the user to add values when checking the values.

After you've created the attribute, you have to assign some values to your pages. In the **Sitemap** dialog, click on a portfolio page and edit its properties as shown in the following screenshot:

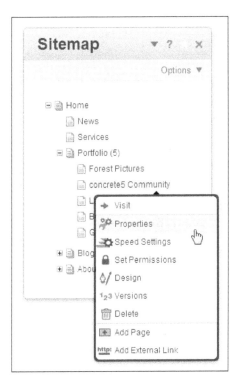

In the **Properties** dialog, change to the second tab **Custom Properties**, and scroll to the bottom to add the new attribute tags. If you scroll back to the top, you'll see an input box where you can start typing a tag. concrete5 will automatically suggest the values that match the values you've previously entered. Save the changes and assign tags to every portfolio page.

Creating a page list filter template

Our block template is going to have the following structure at the end:

The `jquery.quicksand.js` file can be downloaded from `https://github.com/` `razorjack/quicksand/raw/master/jquery.quicksand.js`. You'll have to create all the other files by yourself.

Let's start with the `view.php` file, which is a copy of the `view.php` file in `/concrete/` `blocks/page_list` but was reduced to keep the code a bit shorter and easier to read:

```php
<?php
defined('C5_EXECUTE') or die('Access Denied.');
$rssUrl = $showRss ? $controller->getRssUrl($b) : '';
$th = Loader::helper('text');
?>

<div class="navbar">
  <div class="navbar-inner">
    <ul class="ccm-page-list-quicksand-filter nav nav-pills"
id="quicksand-filter-<?php echo $bID ?>">
      <li data-filter="all"><a href="#">all</a></li>
        <?php
          Loader::model('attribute/type');
          Loader::model('attribute/categories/collection');

          $cak = CollectionAttributeKey::getByHandle('tags');
          $satc = $cak->getController();
          $values = $satc->getOptions();
          foreach ($values as $v) {
            echo "<li data-filter=\"{$v->value}\"><a
href=\"#\">{$v->value}</a></li>";
          }
        ?>
    </ul>
```

```
  </div>
</div>

<ul class="ccm-page-list-quicksand" id="quicksand-content-<?php echo
$bID ?>">
  <?php
  foreach ($pages as $page):
    $title = $th->entities($page->getCollectionName());
    $url = $nh->getLinkToCollection($page);
    $target = ($page->getCollectionPointerExternalLink() != '' &&
$page->openCollectionPointerExternalLinkInNewWindow()) ? '_blank'
: $page->getAttribute('nav_target');
    $target = empty($target) ? '_self' : $target;
    $id = $page->getCollectionID();
    $tags = str_replace("\n", " ", $page->getAttribute('tags'));

    echo "<li class=\"btn\" data-id=\"{$id}\" data-
class=\"{$tags}\"><a href=\"{$url}\"
target=\"{$target}\">{$title}</a></li>";
  endforeach;
  ?>
</ul>

<div style="clear: both"></div>
```

The first highlighted code lines are responsible for fetching the available tags. We could have hardcoded this, but since your customer might add some tags himself, using this slightly more complicated but dynamic solution is probably superior.

We also want to display our pages in boxes and therefore need to put the following code in the view.css file:

```
ccm-page-list-quicksand {
  margin: 0;
  list-style-type: none;
}
ccm-page-list-quicksand li {
  display: block;
  width: 70px;
  height: 50px;
  float: left;
  margin: 10px;
}
```

The last piece is the `view.js` file where we listen for clicks on the filter buttons and call quicksand to filter the pages accordingly. Remember that the `jquery.quicksand.js` file is automatically loaded because its file extension is `.js` and is located in the `js` directory. The following is the complete JavaScript code:

```
$(document).ready(function() {
    // clone the structure needed for quicksand
    var $holder = $('.ccm-page-list-quicksand');
    var $items = $holder.clone();

    $('.ccm-page-list-quicksand-filter > li').click(function(e) {
        // get the filter value from the current button
        var $filterType = $(this).data('filter');

        if ($filterType == 'all') {
            // get all available items
            var $filteredData = $items.find('li');
        }
        else {
            // find all elements matching our filter
            var $filteredData = $items.find('li[data-class~=' +
$filterType + ']');
        }

        // call quicksand to filter items
        $holder.quicksand($filteredData);
        return false;
    });
});
```

If you have created all these files, go to the portfolio page and insert a new page list. Please note that our template doesn't support pagination, you therefore have to leave the field with the number of pages empty and keep the checkbox for the pagination unticked. You might also want to use the portfolio page as the parent element of the list to make sure that only the portfolio pages are shown in the list.

After you've added the block, click on it again and change `Custom Template` to `Quicksand`. Once you've confirmed this change, you'll see the final list which should look like the following screenshot:

Working with picture attributes and creating thumbnails

We've used `$page->getAttribute('tags')` to get the list of assigned tags on a page. Getting a picture is very similar — assuming that we have an attribute with the handle `picture`, we could use something like the following code to show a picture in the page list:

```
$file = $page->getAttribute('picture');
if ($file instanceof File) {
   echo '<img src="' . $file->getURL() . '" alt=""/>';
}
```

The preceding code displays the picture the way it has been uploaded. Sometimes, it's better to make sure the picture doesn't exceed a certain size by restricting its width and height. Have a look at the following code, which does the same as the previous code but limits the width to 200 and height to 150 pixels:

```
$ih = Loader::helper('image');
$file = $page->getAttribute('picture');
if ($file instanceof File) {
   $ih->outputThumbnail($file, 200, 150);
}
```

Just play around with this and you'll quickly become familiar with the attributes, a very powerful and flexible tool.

Summary

In this chapter, we've reached the limit of complexity we need to create themes. Customizing block templates isn't always necessary, but it's sometimes the icing on the cake. If you look around the concrete5 marketplace, you'll find a bunch of themes that don't contain any block templates; but those that are popular usually ship with a few block templates.

Even if you don't intend to distribute your themes in the marketplace, block templates might still be required to suit the needs of either you or your customer. If you don't have a lot of PHP experience, this part can be a bit tricky; but keep in mind that block templates can often be reused in different projects. Spending some time to build a set of block templates you know how to work with can give you a lot of benefits, especially if you intend to develop your business.

There's one more chapter in which we'll make sure that all of these things work on a device with a smaller screen as well, adding the final piece to make a quality theme.

6
Responsive Themes

There was a time when the Internet was only available on computers; things started to change slowly but are now taking up speed. There are even countries such as Japan where more people access the Internet on a mobile device than on a computer.

It might not be the same for your customers yet, but mobile devices are certainly something you should consider when building a website in 2013. There are several approaches to do this; lately it's the word **responsive** that has gained a lot of popularity. A responsive layout aims to provide a viewing experience that adapts to the device the website visitor is using by scaling, hiding, or adding certain elements to match the resolution of the device screen.

In this chapter we'll look at the following things:

- A quick introduction on how to create a completely different layout for mobile devices, or a responsive theme
- The basics behind responsive techniques to make a site work on small screen devices
- The changes we have to make to the previously created theme in order to make it responsive
- A custom template for the `autonav` block to create mobile friendly navigation

Responsive or separate mobile websites

There has been a long talk about whether you should create a separate mobile site with a different layout or even different content, or use the standard site and make it work on small-screen devices by using responsive technologies. This is probably a discussion that won't end anytime soon, but it seems like responsive layouts have gained more popularity than technologies related to creating separate mobile sites.

If you intend to show different content on a mobile device, you might want to consider creating a separate site. But keep in mind that only your website's visitors really know what they want. You might have a visitor who is looking for the phone number and nothing else and gets annoyed because he has to scroll down to the contact page, but it could very well be possible that another visitor wants to read more of the content you have on your site.

We're not going to start a long discussion about this; just keep a few things in mind that you might want to think about before you make this decision:

- If you have a separate mobile site, you'll have to detect the device and redirect the user to the correct page. Such a redirection takes a bit of time and might not always work well, as hardware manufacturers release new devices almost daily.

  - There are libraries you can use to detect the browser; a string called **user-agent (UA)** is used to achieve this. You don't have to create that list yourself; you can use a library such as `https://github.com/serbanghita/Mobile-Detect` (which, by the way, is already included in concrete5). But also remember that you might have to update that library in the future to make it work with new devices.

  - You can also access a UA detection service to avoid having to update the library. But don't forget that this also means that you'll have a dependency from your site to a third-party service.

- Is it a notebook, tablet, ultrabook, or subnotebook? A few years back, we only had desktop computers and cell phones with a rather small resolution. In the meantime, we have had all kinds of devices: small notebooks, tablets, and even tablets which connect to a keyboard, making it work like a notebook. Would you want to display a mobile website to a user working with a tablet? What if that user works in his office and has a keyboard attached to the tablet? It's not really clear; and unless you want to conduct a survey, you probably have to make some assumptions.

- Creating and managing a separate site for mobile devices takes time; but don't get this wrong, a responsive layout doesn't come for free either.

Long story short: Think about what you need, ask your customers, and make a decision. Whatever you want to do, concrete5 is the right tool; and even if you make a bad decision, changing it later is also possible without much hassle.

If you want to build a separate mobile theme to use a different layout for mobile devices, there's not much you need to know if you have already read the previous chapters. You'll have to create a second theme and install it. In the screen where you've installed the theme, you can also specify that you want to use a different theme for mobile devices. Have a look at the following screenshot and you should immediately understand it:

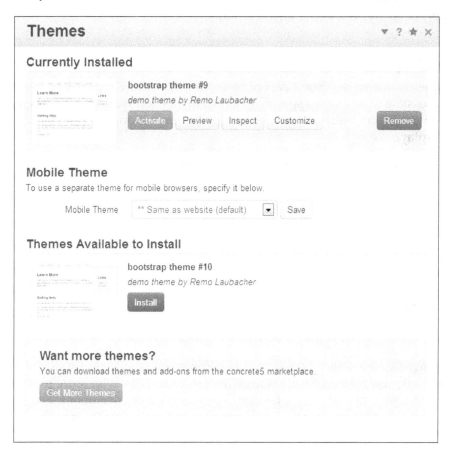

You just have to select the second theme that is to be used for mobile devices and you're done. concrete5 will automatically switch to the correct theme and change the layout of your site for mobile devices. As there isn't more to know, we're just going to talk about responsive layouts.

Responsive techniques

Before we start adding responsive elements to our theme, let's have a look at the basic techniques we're going to work with. When building a site for a device with a small screen, we have to make sure our elements scale relative to the size of the screen.

We might also have to create a different navigation. A wide drop-down navigation would probably not work well on a cell phone.

Media queries

Media queries are an important part of responsive layouts. They are part of CSS to make it possible to add styles specific to a certain media. Media queries can target the output type, screen size, as well as the device orientation, and even the density of the display.

But let's have a look at a simple example before we get lost in theory:

```css
#header {
    background-repeat: no-repeat;
    background-image: url(logo.png);
}

@media print {
    #header {
        display: none;
    }
}
```

The highlighted line in the preceding code snippet makes sure that all the nested styles are only used if the CSS file is used on a printer. To be a bit more precise, it will hide the element with the ID header once you print the document. The same could be achieved by creating two different files and including them with a code as follows:

```html
<link rel="stylesheet" media="all" href="normal.css" />
<link rel="stylesheet" media="print" href="print.css" />
```

It's not always clear whether you want to create a separate CSS file or not. Using too many CSS files might slow down the loading process a bit, but having one big file might make it a bit messier to handle it. Having a separate print CSS is something you'll see rather often while screen resolution dependent queries are usually in the main CSS file.

Here's another example where we use the screen width to break a two columns layout into a single column layout if the screen gets smaller. The following screenshot shows you the layout on an average desktop computer as well as on a tablet:

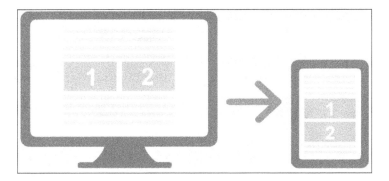

The HTML code we need for our example looks as follows:

```
<div class="box">1</div>
<div class="box">2</div>
```

The CSS including the media queries could be as follows:

```
.box {
    width: 46%;
    padding: 2%;
    float: left;
}

@media all and (max-width: 1023px) {
    .box {
        width: 96%;
        float: none;
    }
}
```

By default, each box has a width of 46 percent and a padding of 2 percent on each side, adding up to a total width of 50 percent. If you look at the highlighted line, you can see a media query relevant to all media types but with a restriction to a maximum width of 1023 pixels. This means that if you view the page on a device with a screen width less than 1023 pixels, the nested CSS styles will be used. In the preceding example, we're overriding the default width of 46 percent with 96 percent. In combination with the 2 percent padding that is still there, we're going to stretch the box to the width of the screen.

Checking the maximum width can achieve a lot already, but there are different queries as well. Here are a few queries that could be useful:

- The following query matches the iPad but only if the orientation is landscape. You could also check the portrait mode by using `orientation: portrait`.

  ```
  @media screen and (device-width: 768px) and (device-height:
  1024px) and (orientation: landscape)
  ```

- If you want to display content specific for a high-resolution screen such as a retina display, use this:

  ```
  @media all and (-webkit-min-device-pixel-ratio: 2)
  ```

- Instead of checking the maximum width, you can also do it the other way round and check the minimum width. The following query could be used to use styles only used in a normal-sized screen:

  ```
  @media screen and (min-width: 1224px)
  ```

There are a lot more variables you can check in a media query. You can find a nicely arranged list of queries including a testing application on the following site:

```
http://cssmediaqueries.com/
```

Try to get an overview of what's possible; but don't worry, you'll hardly ever need more than four media queries.

How to scale pictures

We've seen how you can check the device type in a few different ways, and also used this to change a two-column layout into a single-column layout. This allows you to rearrange the layout elements; but what happens to pictures if the container, in which the picture is located, changes size?

If you look at the following screen, you can see a mock-up where the picture has to change its width from 1000 pixels to 700 pixels:

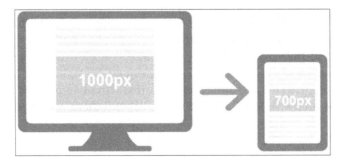

Look at the code that follows:

```
<div id="container">
    <img src="picture.jpg" width="1000" height="400">
</div>
```

Assuming the HTML code looks like this, if we would add a responsive media query that resizes the container to match the width of the screen, we've to cut off a part of the picture. What we want to do is to scale the picture within the container to have the same or a smaller size than the container.

The following CSS snippet can be added to any CSS file to make your pictures scale nicely in a responsive layout:

```
img {
    max-width: 100%;
    height: auto;
}
```

Once you've added this little snippet, your picture will never get bigger than its parent container. The property `max-width` is pretty obvious; it restricts the maximum size. But why is `height: auto` necessary? If you look at the preceding HTML code, you can see that our picture has a fixed width and height. If we'd only specify `max-width` and look at the picture on a screen with a width of 500 pixels, we'd get a picture with the dimensions 500 x 400 pixels. The picture would be distorted. To avoid this, we specify `height: auto;` to make sure the height stays in relation to the width of the picture.

Pictures on high-density screens

If you printed some of your graphic ideas on a paper and not just displayed them on a computer screen, you'll probably have heard of **pixels per inch** (ppi) and **dots per inch** (dpi) before. It's a measure you can use to determine the number of pixels per inch. You'll get a higher density and more details if you have more pixels or dots per inch.

You might have read about retina screens; those displays have a density of around 300 dpi, about twice as much as an average computer monitor. You don't have to, but it's nice if you also make sure that you give owners of such a device the chance to look at high-quality pictures.

What's necessary to deliver a high-quality picture to a retina screen? Some of you might think that you have to save an image with more ppi; but that's not what you should do when creating a retina-ready site. Devices with a retina display simply ignore the pixels per inch information stored in an image. However, the dimension of your images matters.

A picture saved for a retina display should have exactly twice the size of the original image. You could use an SVG picture instead but you still have to use a fallback picture because SVG isn't supported as well as image formats like PNG. In theory, SVG would be even better because it is vector-based and scales perfectly in any resolution.

Enough theory, let's look at an example that uses CSS to display a different image for a retina display:

```
#logo {
    background-image: url(logo.png);
    background-size: 400px 150px;
    width: 400px;
    height: 150px;
}

@media all screen and (-webkit-min-device-pixel-ratio: 2) {
    #logo {
        background-image: url(logo@2x.png);
    }
}
```

We've got an HTML element `<div id="logo"></div>` where we display a background picture to show our logo. If you look at the media query, you can see that we're checking a variable called `-webkit-min-device-pixel-ratio` to detect a high-resolution display. In case the display has a pixel ratio of 2 or higher, we're using an alternative picture that is twice the size. But note the width and height of the container stays the same.

What alternatives are there? As we quickly mentioned, a vector-based format such as SVG would have some benefits but isn't supported on IE7 and IE8. However, you can still use SVG. But you have to make sure that there's a fallback image for those two browsers. Have a look at the following code:

```
<!--[if lte IE 8]>
    <img src="logo.png" width="200" height="50" />
<![endif]-->
<!--[if gt IE 8]>
    <img src="logo.svg" width="200" height="50" />
<![endif]-->
<!--[if !IE]>-->
    <img src="logo.svg" width="200" height="50" />
<!--<![endif]-->
```

In the preceding code, we're using conditional tags to make sure that the old versions of Internet Explorer use the logo saved as PNG, but switch to SVG for modern browsers. It takes a bit more effort because you have to work with vectors and still have to save it as a PNG file, but if you want to make sure your logo or illustrations are nicely displayed when zoomed, use this trick.

Working with SVG is an option, but there's another vector-based solution that you might want to use in some situations. A simple text is always rendered using vectors. No matter what font size you're using, it will always have sharp edges. Most people probably think about letters, numbers, and punctuation marks when they think about fonts, but there are icon fonts as well. Also keep in mind that you can create your own icon web font too. Check this site: `http://fontello.com/`, which is a nice tool that allows you to select the icons you need and use it as a web font. You can also create your very own icon web font from scratch; check out the following link for a detailed tutorial:

`http://www.webdesignerdepot.com/2012/01/how-to-make-your-own-icon-webfont/`

One last word before we continue; Retina screens are relatively new. It's therefore no surprise that some of the specifications to create a perfect retina layout are still drafts. The Web is a fast moving place; expect some changes and new features to insert an image with multiple sources and more vector features.

Viewport on small-screen devices

If you read about responsive design earlier, you've probably seen the `viewport` meta tag. Don't worry if you haven't heard of it before; there's nothing complicated about it, but it's important to know.

On a site without a `viewport` meta tag, the browser will try to scale the page properly. This can have the effect that the text is very tiny and impossible to read. Mobile browsers are trying to display a page in the best way possible, but often fail because the site isn't responsive. Just imagine what a browser should do if the page's content is very wide. It can either display a shrunken down version or cut off a part on the right-hand side. Both ways aren't very nice, but a shrunken down page might still be better, especially if you keep in mind that almost every touch device has a rather intuitive zoom function.

This is what happens on a non-responsive site; but we're going to make it responsive and therefore have a few more options. Even if your site is responsive, a mobile browser can still have a hard time determining the best default scaling. That's the reason why you might want to use a meta tag called `viewport`; this will make it possible to set some properties related to the default scaling and viewport of your site.

Let's look at the meta tag that is most commonly used, and which might actually be enough for your site:

```
<meta name="viewport" content="width=device-width, initial-scale=1.0">
```

The `viewport` meta tag can have several options, each separated with a comma. You might see some `viewport` tags where a semicolon is used instead. This works on newer browsers, but isn't officially supported.

Let's look at both properties:

- `width=device-width`: This will make sure that the page is displayed with the width of the device by default. Your screen has a width of 640 pixels; so does the default viewport. Fixed numbers can be used as well, for example, `width=500`.

- `initial-scale=1.0`: The scaling your site will use by default. `1.0` means 100 percent, `0.7` means 70 percent.

If you look at the next screenshot, you can see a mobile phone mock-up that is 980 pixels wide. The content with the picture has a width of 490 pixels. If you use the default viewport settings, it will only take a quarter of the available space. If we now specify `width=490`, the device will scale the content to match the size of the picture. That's the most important part to remember when working with the `viewport` meta tag.

There are more properties you might want to have a look at, but make sure you test the final result. Using `maximum-scale=1` and `minimum-scale=1` would disable the zooming function on the device; something you sometimes see but hardly ever want.

- `minimum-scale=0.5`: Scaling below 50 percent isn't possible
- `maximum-scale=1.5`: Scaling higher than 150 percent isn't possible
- `user-scalable=no`: Scaling by the user is disabled
- `height=device-height`: Set the height of the viewport to height of the device

Navigation for small screens

If you want to be able to navigate through your site on a mobile device, you'll probably have to make your navigation behave differently. A full-fledged drop-down menu simply doesn't have enough space to be displayed on a cell phone.

Let's start with a simple example by looking at the next screenshot. It shows a horizontal navigation that has too many items for a mobile phone or tablet. Making it responsive could be as easy as making it vertical.

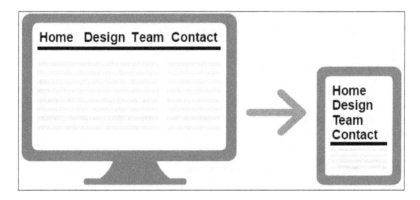

If you're using a drop-down navigation, you'll have to display several levels of your site's structure. Showing all available pages like a sitemap at the top of the page when viewed with a mobile phone is probably a bit too much. You wouldn't want your site's visitors to scroll down to see the actual content.

A frequently used way to improve this is to hide the navigation by default and reveal it after a click on an icon with three bars:

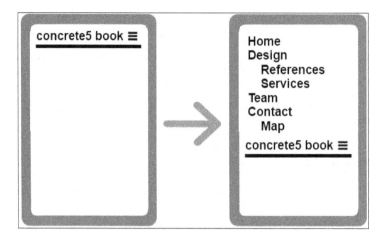

This is, of course, not the only way to do this, but it's the one that works well. It's also what we're trying to integrate in our theme.

Responsive layout implementation in concrete5

In this part, we'll add everything that's necessary to make the previously created theme ready for small-screen devices. To do this, we'll have to add some CSS files and also create a new `autonav` block template to create a mobile-friendly navigation.

Responsive bootstrap CSS

The bootstrap framework we've worked with offers a wide variety of options to create a responsive layout. The most important part is a CSS file you can find in the bootstrap archive you've downloaded. Before you start making modifications, create a new copy of our theme by copying `bootstrap9` to `bootstrap10`. If you don't have the bootstrap ZIP file anymore, go to `http://twitter.github.com/bootstrap/` and download the current version. From that ZIP file, extract `bootstrap-responsive.min.css` and copy it to `themes/bootstrap10/css/bootstrap-responsive.min.css`.

Next, we have to make sure this file is included in our theme. Open `elements/header.php` and insert the highlighted line:

```php
<?php defined('C5_EXECUTE') or die('Access Denied.') ?>


<!DOCTYPE html>
<html lang="en">
    <head>
        <link rel="stylesheet" media="screen" type="text/css"
href="<?php echo $this->getThemePath() ?>/css/bootstrap.min.css"
/>
        <link rel="stylesheet" media="screen" type="text/css"
href="<?php echo $this->getThemePath() ?>/css/bootstrap-responsive.
min.css" />
        <link rel="stylesheet" media="screen" type="text/css"
href="<?php echo $this->getStylesheet('main.css') ?>" />
        <link rel="stylesheet" media="screen" type="text/css"
href="<?php echo $this->getThemePath() ?>/typography.css" />

        <meta name="viewport" content="width=device-width, initial-
scale=1.0">

        <!-- Le HTML5 shim, for IE6-8 support of HTML5 elements -->
        <!--[if lt IE 9]>
            <script src="http://html5shim.googlecode.com/svn/trunk/
html5.js"></script>
        <![endif]-->

        <?php Loader::element('header_required'); ?>
            . . .
```

If you install and activate this theme, you can already see a slightly different behavior on your site. If you open a page with two columns and make your browser's window smaller, the columns get smaller. That's nothing new; but if you make the window even smaller, you'll notice that the columns are gone. The two boxes are vertically aligned now.

You can see that the grid system we're using works nicely in a responsive layout. If you keep using the CSS classes `span*` and `offset*`, you have already mastered one part of responsive layouts. If you want to have another look at the grid system, the official documentation is probably the best place for it:

```
http://twitter.github.com/bootstrap/scaffolding.html#fluidGridSystem
```

Twitter bootstrap has another small utility we want to look at. If you include the responsive CSS, you'll get a number of classes you can use to hide and show content depending on the device. Have a look at the following code snippet:

```
<div class="visible-phone">
    content only visible on phone
</div>

<div class="hidden-phone">
    content hidden on phone
</div>
```

As you can see, we're using two classes, `visible-phone` and `hidden-phone`, to make some content available only on a phone and hide the second box on a phone. You can find a complete list as well as a bit more information on the following page:

`http://twitter.github.com/bootstrap/scaffolding.html#responsive`

These classes can also be used in the editing interface. Imagine you want to display the contact information on top of the home page when the page is viewed on a mobile phone, and only there, add a new content block with all the information you want to display. After you've added this block, click on it again and select the **Design** item as shown in the following screenshot:

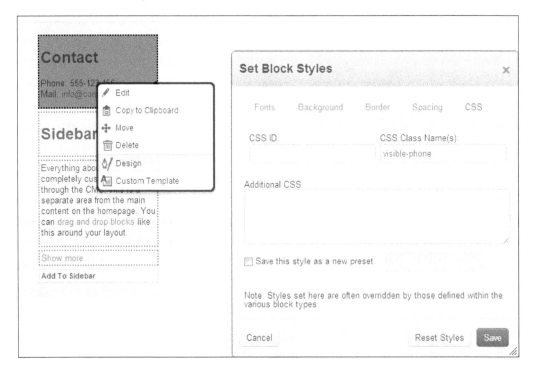

In the last registered CSS, you can specify your own CSS classes. In our case, simply enter `visible-phone` and the content will be exclusively displayed on a phone.

Responsive drop-down navigation

As you might have expected, bootstrap has a solution to create a responsive drop-down navigation in no time. All we have to do is change the HTML output a bit and include a JavaScript file..

First, you have to add another file from Twitter bootstrap. From the ZIP file you've already downloaded, extract the JavaScript `bootstrap.min.js` and place it in `themes/bootstrap10/js/bootstrap.min.js`.

We're still in the same file, `elements/header.php`. The complete file we need to make our design responsive has to look as the following; the changes mentioned earlier are in it as well:

```php
<?php defined('C5_EXECUTE') or die('Access Denied.') ?>

<!DOCTYPE html>
<html lang="en">
    <head>
        <link rel="stylesheet" media="screen" type="text/css"
href="<?php echo $this->getThemePath() ?>/css/bootstrap.min.css" />
        <link rel="stylesheet" media="screen" type="text/css"
href="<?php echo $this->getThemePath() ?>/css/bootstrap-responsive.
min.css" />
        <link rel="stylesheet" media="screen" type="text/css"
href="<?php echo $this->getStylesheet('main.css') ?>" />
        <link rel="stylesheet" media="screen" type="text/css"
href="<?php echo $this->getThemePath() ?>/typography.css" />

        <meta name="viewport" content="width=device-width, initial-
scale=1.0">

        <!-- Le HTML5 shim, for IE6-8 support of HTML5 elements -->
        <!--[if lt IE 9]>
          <script src="http://html5shim.googlecode.com/svn/trunk/
html5.js"></script>
        <![endif]-->

        <?php Loader::element('header_required'); ?>
```

```php
<?php
// get background from current page
$backgroundPicture = $c->getAttribute('background');

// no picture found, try to get it from the home page
if (!$backgroundPicture instanceof File) {
    $homePage = Page::getByID(HOME_CID);
    $backgroundPicture = $homePage-
    >getAttribute('background');
}

// call supersized if picture found
if ($backgroundPicture instanceof File) {
    echo '<script src="' . $this->getThemePath() .
    '/js/supersized.core.3.2.1.min.js"></script>';
    echo "
        <script>
        $(document).ready(function() {
            $.supersized({slides : [ {image :
            '{$backgroundPicture->getURL()}'} ]});

        });
        </script>
        ";
}

// add bootstrap JavaScript for our drop down navigation
echo '<script src="' . $this->getThemePath() .
'/js/bootstrap.min.js"></script>';
?>

</head>

<body>

    <div id="wrapper">
        <nav class="navbar">
            <div class="navbar-inner">
                <div class="container">
                    <a class="btn btn-navbar" data-
                    toggle="collapse" data-target=".nav-collapse">
                        <span class="icon-bar"></span>
                        <span class="icon-bar"></span>
```

```
            <span class="icon-bar"></span>
        </a>
        <a class="brand" href="#">concrete5 book</a>
        <div class="nav-collapse">
          <?php
          $bt = BlockType::getByHandle('autonav');
          $bt->controller->displayPages = 'top';
          $bt->controller->orderBy = display_asc';
          $bt->controller->displaySubPages =
          'all';
          $bt->controller->displaySubPageLevels =
          'custom';
          $bt->controller->displaySubPageLevelsNum
          = 2;
          $bt->render('templates/bootstrap');
          ?>
        </div>
      </div>
    </div>
  </nav>

  <div class="container-fluid">
```

The first two highlighted code blocks are the changes we made earlier. One includes the bootstrap-responsive CSS and the other one sets the default responsive viewport.

The last highlighted block contains some new HTML code that is needed to add an icon displayed on small-screen devices. There are three elements with the class icon-bar to create the final icon. There's another element with the btn-navbar and data-target attributes pointing to the navigation to toggle the navigation on a small-screen device.

That's it! Nothing else is needed to make your navigation responsive. If you look at your site on a device with a smaller screen or with a browser window resized to less than 767 pixels, you'll see a layout as shown in the following screenshot. As soon as you click on the icon with the three bars, you'll see the navigation.

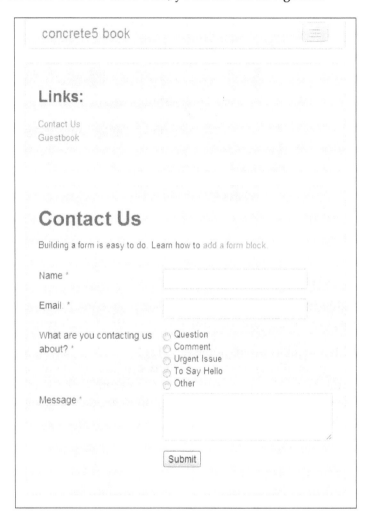

Responsive sidebar navigation

Another approach to make the navigation work on small devices is to display a second navigation in a sidebar. We're going to use the same button with three bars; but instead of moving the navigation down from the top, we're going to slide it over the content from the left.

This could be useful not only for a navigation, but also to display frequently searched information. If you have a lot of visitors on mobile phones looking for your phone number, why not place it where it's always easy to find? However, we're going to add another sitemap-like structure. The final result will look like the following screenshot when viewed on a tablet or a phone:

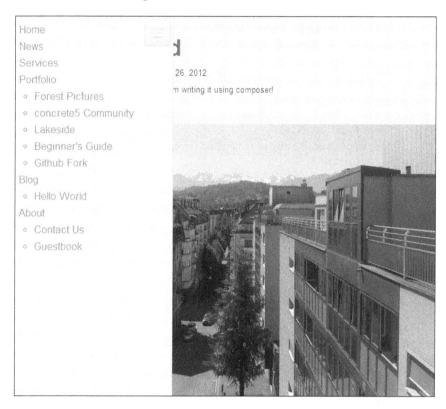

As always, create a new clone of your previous theme, bootstrap10, and name it bootstrap11. Make sure you install and activate it.

We're going to work with some functions from bootstrap to avoid having to write our own JavaScript code. All we need is a bit of HTML and some CSS to style our sidebar. In your new theme, open elements/header.php and make sure it looks like the following code; all changes are highlighted:

```php
<?php defined('C5_EXECUTE') or die('Access Denied.') ?>

<!DOCTYPE html>
<html lang="en">
    <head>
```

```php
        <link rel="stylesheet" media="screen" type="text/css"
href="<?php echo $this->getThemePath() ?>/css/bootstrap.min.css" />
        <link rel="stylesheet" media="screen" type="text/css"
href="<?php echo $this->getThemePath() ?>/css/bootstrap-responsive.
css" />
        <link rel="stylesheet" media="screen" type="text/css"
href="<?php echo $this->getStylesheet('main.css') ?>" />
        <link rel="stylesheet" media="screen" type="text/css"
href="<?php echo $this->getThemePath() ?>/typography.css" />

        <meta name="viewport" content="width=device-width, initial-
scale=1.0">

        <!-- Le HTML5 shim, for IE6-8 support of HTML5 elements -->
        <!--[if lt IE 9]>
          <script src="http://html5shim.googlecode.com/svn/trunk/
html5.js"></script>
        <![endif]-->

        <?php Loader::element('header_required'); ?>

        <?php
        // get background from current page
        $backgroundPicture = $c->getAttribute('background');

        // no picture found, try to get it from the home page
        if (!$backgroundPicture instanceof File) {
            $homePage = Page::getByID(HOME_CID);
            $backgroundPicture = $homePage-
            >getAttribute('background');
        }

        // call supersized if picture found
        if ($backgroundPicture instanceof File) {
            echo '<script src="' . $this->getThemePath() .
            '/js/supersized.core.3.2.1.min.js"></script>';
            echo "
                <script>
                $(document).ready(function() {
                    $.supersized({slides : [ {image :
                    '{$backgroundPicture->getURL()}'} ]});

                });
                </script>
                ";
        }
```

```php
// add bootstrap JavaScript for our drop down navigation
echo '<script src="' . $this->getThemePath() .
'/js/bootstrap.min.js"></script>';

// add margin to mobile navigation if editing toolbar is
visible
$p = new Permissions($c);
if ($p->canWrite()) {
    echo "<style>
    #sidebar-nav {
        top: 50px;
    }
    </style>";
}?>
```

```html
</head>

<body>

    <div id="sidebar-nav" class="visible-phone visible-tablet">
        <div id="sidebar-nav-collapse">
            <?php
            $bt = BlockType::getByHandle('autonav');
            $bt->controller->displayPages = 'top';
            $bt->controller->orderBy = 'display_asc';
            $bt->controller->displaySubPages = 'all';
            $bt->controller->displaySubPageLevels = 'custom';
            $bt->controller->displaySubPageLevelsNum = 2;
            $bt->render('view');
            ?>
        </div>
        <div id="sidebar-nav-toggle">
            <a class="btn" data-toggle="dropdown" data-
target="#sidebar-nav-collapse">
                <span class="icon-bar"></span>
                <span class="icon-bar"></span>
                <span class="icon-bar"></span>
            </a>
        </div>
        <div class="clearfix"></div>
    </div>

    <div id="wrapper">
```

```
<nav class="navbar hidden-tablet hidden-phone">
    <div class="navbar-inner">
        <?php
        $bt = BlockType::getByHandle('autonav');
        $bt->controller->displayPages = 'top';
        $bt->controller->orderBy = 'display_asc';
        $bt->controller->displaySubPages = 'all';
        $bt->controller->displaySubPageLevels = 'custom';
        $bt->controller->displaySubPageLevelsNum = 2;
        $bt->render('templates/bootstrap');
        ?>
    </div>
</nav>

<div class="container-fluid">
```

As you can see, the container with the ID `sidebar-nav-collapse` contains some code to print a page structure up to the second level using the `autonav` block. We've hardcoded this in our template because we still don't want our editors to change the navigation. The parent container, `sidebar-nav`, has two CSS classes: `visible-phone` and `visible-tablet`. By using these bootstrap classes, we can make sure that the sidebar is only visible on phones and tablets.

Our button consists of three bars like before, but the action is a bit different. If you look closely, you can see two attributes specific to bootstrap: `data-toggle` and `data-target`. For `data-toggle`, we're using the value `dropdown`. By using this value, we'll get a class called `open` on our target element. We can then use this class to hide or show the actual navigation. We could have used some custom JavaScript instead of these two attributes to have a bit more flexibility, but if you aren't picky this is more than enough.

The new sidebar needs to have some style as well. Open `main.css` and insert, not replace, the following content:

```
...
#sidebar-nav {
    position: fixed;
    top: 0;
    left: 0;
    height: 100%;
    z-index: 500;
    background-color: #fafafa;
    border: 1px solid #d4d4d4;
    -webkit-border-radius: 4px;
        -moz-border-radius: 4px;
```

```
                        border-radius: 4px;
}
#sidebar-nav .icon-bar {
  display: block;
  width: 20px;
  height: 3px;
  margin-bottom: 3px;
  background-color: #f5f5f5;
  -webkit-border-radius: 1px;
     -moz-border-radius: 1px;
          border-radius: 1px;
  -webkit-box-shadow: 0 1px 0 rgba(0, 0, 0, 0.25);
     -moz-box-shadow: 0 1px 0 rgba(0, 0, 0, 0.25);
          box-shadow: 0 1px 0 rgba(0, 0, 0, 0.25);
}
@media (max-width: 979px) {
    body {
        margin: 0;
        padding: 0 0 0 50px;
    }
}
#sidebar-nav-collapse {
    float: left;
    width: 200px;
    padding: 5px;
    font-size: 130%;
    display: none;
}
#sidebar-nav-collapse li {
    margin: 6px 0;
}
#sidebar-nav-toggle {
    float: left;
    width: 50px;
}
#sidebar-nav-toggle .btn {
    float: left;
    padding: 10px;
    margin: 4px;
}
#sidebar-nav-collapse.open {
    display: block;
}
```

Let's have a quick look at three important elements in this new CSS block:

- `position: fixed`: The value `fixed` isn't supported on older browsers; but mobile devices support this well. We use it to make sure the sidebar, including its button, stays visible even if we scroll down.

- `@media (max-width: 979px)`: As soon as we have a small screen, our sidebar becomes visible due to the two classes `visible-phone` and `visible-tablet`. When the sidebar is visible, it would overlap our content and probably make it hard to read. We're using a media query that matches all screens smaller than 979 pixels and add padding on the left-hand side of our padding. By doing this, we can make sure the sidebar is docked on the left-hand side of the page but doesn't overlap anything.

- `#sidebar-nav-collapse.open`: As previously mentioned, by using `data-toggle="dropdown"`, the bootstrap frameworks adds a class called `open` to our target elements. We can use this class to make the content of our sidebar visible.

We had to write a bit of code to achieve this, but if you compare this solution to other ways of making a responsive navigation, you'll see that it's a pretty easy approach. The HTML code is simple and easy to style with CSS.

Summary

Congratulations, you've reached the end of the book! If you have carefully read everything up to this point, you should have the knowledge to use your experience with HTML and CSS to turn your layout into a concrete5 theme in no time.

In this chapter, we've looked at the basics you have to know if you want to make sure that your website works on different devices such as mobile phones and even tablets. This is mostly related to HTML and CSS, but as you've seen, concrete5 gives you a lot of freedom when building a theme. We've also cleared the hurdle of making your site responsive almost effortlessly. Adding CSS media queries, special meta tags and more isn't a problem in concrete5.

I hope you've enjoyed this book and are ready to create great concrete5 themes. If you have any problems, there's an active support forum available at `http://www.concrete5.org/community/forums/`. If you found any mistakes in this book, please report them at `http://www.c5book.com`.

Index

Symbols

$this->action('send') 85
$this->controller->getTask() 85
$th->sanitize($message) 85

A

anatomy, of block 40, 41
anatomy, of page 39
architecture, concrete5
  file structure 34
  MVC 37
area 13
Auto-Nav block 11

B

background picture
  attribute, assigning to page type 75, 76
  attribute, creating for holding picture 74, 75
  building 73
  selecting 76
basic package installer 46-48
block properties
  finding 68-70
blocks
  about 11
  adding 14
  default blocks 11
  Edit menu item 15
  options 14
  overriding, in packages 102
  putting, in templates 67
  updating 15, 16
  using 11

block templates
  creating, for content block using
    fancyBox 99-101
  overriding 95-98
  with CSS and JavaScript 99
  working with 96
Blog Date Archive block 13
bootstrap 51
bootstrap theme
  creating 52
  CSS files, adding 58
  installing 57
  page type template, adding 52
  shared footer, creating 56
  shared header, creating 54, 55
  theme thumbnail, adding 57

C

caching 37
concrete5
  about 5
  architecture 33
  area 13
  block, overriding in packages 102
  blocks 11
  block templates, overriding 95-97
  caching 37
  changes, publishing 16
  content, editing 9, 10
  content structures 22
  CSS files, adding to theme 58
  demo site, running 5
  events 44
  files, managing 18
  helpers 42, 43

Slideshow block 12
stack
  about 20
  block, adding 21
  creating 20
Survey block 12

T

Tags block 12
templates, for page types 70
test_form.php 84
theme
  attributes, working with 77-79
  background picture, by page attribute 73
  blocks, putting in templates 67, 68
  global areas 66
  header area, replacing with global area 66
  number of blocks per area, specifying 71-73
  page-specific variables 79
  templates, for page types 70, 71

TinyMCE 15
typography.css
  adding 59, 60

U

UA detection service 118
update process, concrete5 35
URL Slug field 30
user-agent 118

V

Video Player block 12
viewport on small-screen devices 125-127

Y

YouTube Video block 12

Thank you for buying
Creating concrete5 Themes

About Packt Publishing

Packt, pronounced 'packed', published its first book "*Mastering phpMyAdmin for Effective MySQL Management*" in April 2004 and subsequently continued to specialize in publishing highly focused books on specific technologies and solutions.

Our books and publications share the experiences of your fellow IT professionals in adapting and customizing today's systems, applications, and frameworks. Our solution based books give you the knowledge and power to customize the software and technologies you're using to get the job done. Packt books are more specific and less general than the IT books you have seen in the past. Our unique business model allows us to bring you more focused information, giving you more of what you need to know, and less of what you don't.

Packt is a modern, yet unique publishing company, which focuses on producing quality, cutting-edge books for communities of developers, administrators, and newbies alike. For more information, please visit our website: www.packtpub.com.

About Packt Open Source

In 2010, Packt launched two new brands, Packt Open Source and Packt Enterprise, in order to continue its focus on specialization. This book is part of the Packt Open Source brand, home to books published on software built around Open Source licences, and offering information to anybody from advanced developers to budding web designers. The Open Source brand also runs Packt's Open Source Royalty Scheme, by which Packt gives a royalty to each Open Source project about whose software a book is sold.

Writing for Packt

We welcome all inquiries from people who are interested in authoring. Book proposals should be sent to author@packtpub.com. If your book idea is still at an early stage and you would like to discuss it first before writing a formal book proposal, contact us; one of our commissioning editors will get in touch with you.

We're not just looking for published authors; if you have strong technical skills but no writing experience, our experienced editors can help you develop a writing career, or simply get some additional reward for your expertise.

concrete5 Beginner's Guide

ISBN: 978-1-84951-428-6   Paperback: 320 pages

Create and customize your own website with the
concrete5 Beginner's Guide

1.   Follow the creation of a sample site, through
     the installation, configuration, and deployment
     of a Concrete5 site

2.   Use themes and add-ons to create a
     personalized site

3.   Ideal introduction to using the Concrete5 CMS

4.   Part of Packt's Beginner's Guide series – lots of
     practical examples, screenshots, and less of the
     waffle

Drupal 7 Themes

ISBN: 978-1-84951-276-3   Paperback: 320 pages

Create new themes for your Drupal 7 site with a clean
layout and powerful CSS styling

1.   Learn to create new Drupal 7 themes

2.   No experience of Drupal theming required

3.   Discover techniques and tools for creating and
     modifying themes

4.   The first book to guide you through the new
     elements and themes available in Drupal 7

Please check **www.PacktPub.com** for information on our titles

jQuery UI Themes Beginner's Guide

ISBN: 978-1-84951-044-8   Paperback: 268 pages

Create new themes for your jQuery site with this step-by-step guide

1. Learn the details of the jQuery UI theme framework by example

2. No prior knowledge of jQuery UI or theming frameworks is necessary

3. The CSS structure is explained in an easy-to-understand and approachable way

4. Numerous examples, no unnecessary long explanations, lots of screenshots and diagrams

Drupal 7 Multi Sites Configuration

ISBN: 978-1-84951-800-0   Paperback: 100 pages

Run multiple websites from a single instance of Drupal 7

1. Prepare your server for hosting multiple sites

2. Configure and install several sites on one instance of Drupal

3. Manage and share themes and modules across the multi-site configuration

Please check **www.PacktPub.com** for information on our titles